W9-BUJ-965

FAMILY MATTERS

✓

FOOD PROCESSOR HINTS AND TIPS

**Also by Deborah Gray
in the Family Matters series:**

Vegetarian Cooking Made Easy (1990)

FAMILY MATTERS

✓

FOOD PROCESSOR
HINTS AND TIPS

DEBORAH GRAY

WARD LOCK

ACKNOWLEDGEMENTS

Many thanks are due to Moulinex and Ariete for the use of their machines while writing this book. Braun, Magimix and Philips have also been helpful in supplying information about their food processors.

A WARD LOCK BOOK

First published in the UK 1992
by Ward Lock
(a Cassell imprint)
Villiers House
41/47 Strand
LONDON
WC2N 5JE

Copyright © 1992 Ward Lock

All rights reserved. No part of this book
may be reproduced or transmitted
in any form or by any means, electronic
or mechanical including photocopying,
recording or any information storage
or retrieval system, without prior permission
in writing from the
copyright holder and Publisher.

Distributed in Australia
by Capricorn Link (Australia) Pty Ltd
P.O. Box 665, Lane Cove, NSW 2066

British Library Cataloguing in Publication Data

Gray, Deborah
  Food processor hints and tips
  I. Title
  641.589

  ISBN 0–7063–7051–1

Typeset in 11 on 11½ point ITC Garamond Light by
Columns Design and Production Services Ltd, Reading

Printed and bound in Great Britain by
Harper Collins, Glasgow

CONTENTS

Introduction   6

    Choosing a food processor   6

    Looking after your food processor   10

    Safety   11

    Notes for American and Australian   12
      users

A–Z Food Processor Dictionary   14

Index of Recipes   126

INTRODUCTION

The food processor is now a standard piece of kitchen equipment, but many machines sit under-used on the shelf simply because their owners are unaware of how much time and effort they can save. This book aims to expand on the information provided by manufacturer's and to show how the processor should be used for preparing every day foods and recipes. Once the basic way in which the food processor works becomes familiar, you will find the processor really useful in the preparation of many of your favourite recipes, and your friends and family will be impressed by the professional appearance of your cooking.

The book assumes only a standard processor is available and although the sophisticated range of attachments are mentioned, they are not taken for granted.

CHOOSING A FOOD PROCESSOR

There is a wide range of food processors on the market, each with a different assortment of attachments and features, not to mention a wide price differential, so it is important to think about exactly what tasks you anticipate asking of your machine. Before buying a food processor, you need to ask yourself the following questions:

☆ How many people do you cook for? If you normally cook for two or three people then a machine with a small capacity will be suitable. However, if you entertain frequently or cook for a crowd, be sure to buy a machine with a large processing bowl. If you think that your family will expand, err on the generous side.

☆ Are you a baker? Home-made bread is addictive and very easy to prepare. Check the manufacturer's handbook to ensure that the processor can make at least a 375 g/12 oz loaf – better still a 450 g/1 lb loaf. It is frustrating to process amounts smaller than this and overloading the machine will damage the motor or cause it to cut out. If you make large quantities of pastry and big cakes, you should buy a machine with a powerful motor and a large capacity bowl.

☆ Is the food processor your only kitchen aid? If you already have an electric mixer, you may not want to have the whisk attachment, but if you do not have a mixer, the attachment can be a boon.

☆ Do you prepare a lot of salads and vegetables? You may wish to buy a machine with a variable sized slicing blade or one which comes with more than one slicing disc so that you can cut thin slices of cucumber and thick slices of potato. If your family likes chips then a special chipper disc is useful.

Think, too, about the feeder tuber. Some machines have a double socket to make it easier to process slim items such as a single carrot, and a wider section for larger foods. There is also the possibility of purchasing a machine with an optional wide feeder tube that can process whole aubergines and wedges of cabbage.

Look for the machine that directs sliced food down a tube into the bowl of your choice rather than into the fitted bowl; this means no more stopping to empty the bowl as it fills.

☆ Will you make fruit juices? There is no point in buying a machine with a citrus press and a juicer if you do not anticipate using these options. But if you enjoy fresh orange juice, the citrus press is really quick and easy to use.

☆ Do you chop herbs, prepare baby foods or small amounts of sauce? If so, you may wish to opt for a processor that has a small bowl which can be used for tiny quantities. Look for a watertight lid if you want to use the mini-bowl for liquids.

☆ Are you timid with machines? You may feel more comfortable with a variable speed control which enables you to process food slowly or quickly.

Tip
Make sure that the machine you choose has a pulse button as this allows you to process foods in short sharp bursts, so you can control the cutting blades and prevent over-processing.

If all these options make you feel daunted, buy a machine with a suitable capacity and simply a straightforward double bladed knife (used for about 80% of all processing operations), slicing and grating discs and a whisk attachment and you will not go far wrong.

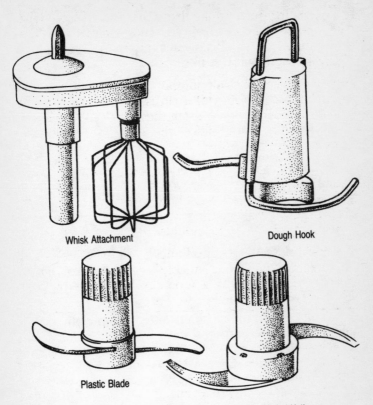

Whisk Attachment

Dough Hook

Plastic Blade

Double Bladed Knife

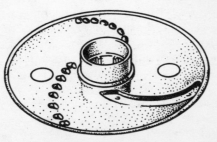

Combined Grating and Slicing Disc

LOOKING AFTER YOUR FOOD PROCESSOR

Depending on what you have used the processor for, rinse the bowl and blades under a running tap to remove the surplus food, then wash in warm soapy water and rinse. Do not leave the double bladed knife in a bowl of washing-up water as it is extremely sharp and could cause a nasty cut. Wash the processor directly after use and you will save time as the foods will not have had a chance to dry on the bowl. Some processor bowls are dishwasher-proof; check with the manufacturer's handbook.

Tip
Use a baby's bottle cleaning brush to reach the nooks and crannies, especially the one inside the knife spool.

Wipe the body of the machine with a damp cloth, never submerge the food processor in water or the motor will be completely ruined. Store the food processor on the work surface with the bowl in place and the double bladed knife fitted. Do not leave it plugged in with the power supply on. You will use the processor much more frequently if it is handy than if you have to get it out of a cupboard and hunt for the attachments.

As you become more familiar with using the food processor, you will find that altering the order in which the ingredients are prepared will prevent you from having to wash the bowl between processes. For instance, always whisk egg whites first as the bowl must be spotless and dry for this operation, then continue with the other steps in the recipe. When making a salad, process the dressing first, then slice the vegetables on top of the dressing.

> ***Tip***
> When chopping vegetables, make sure that the bowl is dry or large pieces will stick to the sides of the bowl and fail to be processed further.

Take care never to overload your food processor or overfill the bowl as this puts a great strain on the motor. Most machines are fitted with an automatic cut out which prevents damaging the motor. The motor will cut out temporarily and restart about one minute later when it has cooled down. Similarly, use the pulse button and on/off switches to control the processor's operation, not the lid. The cut-out function of the lid is there only to avoid the risk of the machine running without the lid securely in place.

The double bladed knife should remain sharp for years. Do not process coffee beans or spices which are very hard – as a general rule, if it is too hard to be chopped with a knife, it is too hard for the processor.

SAFETY

☆ Never be tempted to push food through the feeder tube using the fingers; always use the pusher.

☆ Take great care when handling blades and discs as they are extremely sharp. Keep the double bladed knife fitted to the processor when not in use, or fit the covers that are sometimes supplied. Store all the remaining discs and blades in the storage tray provided or failing that in a box within a drawer to prevent fingers from becoming snagged.

☆ If a piece of food is stuck on the blades or disc, stop the operation and remove carefully with a spatula, not your fingers.

☆ Do not process boiling liquid and even with hot liquid, take care that the pusher is sealing the lid to prevent splashing and burns.

NOTES FOR AMERICAN AND AUSTRALIAN USERS

Please note that the Imperial pint is used throughout i.e. 20 fl oz or 567 ml (rounded up to 600 ml). The standard American measuring cup is 8 fl oz (approx. 240 ml) the Australian 250 ml. The British standard tablespoon has been used, this holds 15 ml compared to the American standard at 14.2 ml and the Australian at 20 ml – use scant or generous measurements as applicable. Teaspoons are all the same at 5 ml.

Note: When following any recipe, use *either* Imperial or Metric measurements; do not mix the two.

LIQUID MEASURES

British Measure	*American Measure*
150 ml/¼ pint	⅔ cup
300 ml/½ pint	1¼ cups
450 ml/¾ pint	scant 2 cups
600 ml/1 pint	2½ cups
1.2 litres/2 pints	5 cups

SOLID MEASURES

British Measure	*American Equivalent*
450 g/1 lb flour	4 cups flour
450 g/1 lb granulated, caster or brown sugar	2 cups granulated, superfine or brown sugar
450 g/1 lb icing sugar	3 cups powdered sugar
450 g/1 lb butter, margarine, or other solid fats	2 cups butter, margarine or other solid fats
25 g/1 oz butter etc.	2 tbs butter etc.
450 g/1 lb grated Cheddar-type cheese	4 cups grated cheese
50 g/2 oz soft breadcrumbs	1 cups soft breadcrumbs
100 g/4 oz dry breadcrumbs	1 cup dry breadcrumbs
75–100 g/3–4 oz button mushrooms	1 cup button mushrooms
150 g/5 oz chopped tomatoes	1 cup chopped tomatoes
450 g/1 lb currant-type fruit	4 cups currant-type fruit
450 g/1 lb berry-type fruit	3½ cups berry-type fruit
150–180 g/5–6 oz raisins, dried chopped fruit	1 cup raisins, dried chopped fruit (nb. sultanas = golden raisins)
150 g/5 oz chopped nuts	1 cup chopped nuts
100 g/4 oz ground almonds	1 cup ground almonds
150 g/5 oz jam/marmalade	1 cup jelly/marmalade

A–Z FOOD PROCESSOR DICTIONARY

A

AIOLI

Double bladed knife

This is a garlic-flavoured mayonnaise. With the motor running, drop 1–4 peeled garlic cloves, depending on how strong you like the taste of garlic, through the feeder tube onto the knife to briefly chop. Then continue to make mayonnaise (page 70) as normal, using lemon juice instead of vinegar.

ALMONDS

Double bladed knife

Almonds can be chopped or ground in the processor using the pulse technique.

See Nuts · Marzipan

APPLES

Double bladed knife
Grating disc
Juice extractor
Slicing disc

Slicing: Perfect evenly sliced apples really enhance the appearance of many tarts, flans and open cakes, and these can be achieved in a matter of minutes in the food processor. Peel the apples using a potato peeler and remove any damaged flesh. Quarter the apples and carefully remove the cores. Feed the prepared apples down the tube pressing with the pusher to ensure an even cut. As apples brown very quickly keep the unsliced, prepared apples in water to which a little lemon juice has been added and transfer cut apple slices to the water as soon as possible. Drain and pat dry before using.

Grating: Use either the coarse grater or cut the prepared apples finely with the double bladed knife.

Puree: For a really smooth apple puree or sauce fit the double bladed knife and process cooked apple for just a few seconds until smooth.

Juice: Fresh apple juice is made using the juice extractor.

Tip
Slice windfall apples, stew lightly with a little sugar and lemon juice and freeze for later use in pies, pancakes and sauces.

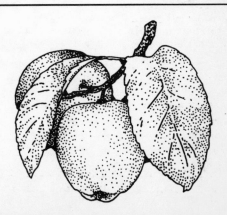

Spiced Apple Cake

Grease and line a deep 18 cm/7 in round cake tin. Place 450 g/1 lb peeled, cored and quartered apples in the bowl and chop into small pieces; set aside. Place in the mixer bowl (without washing) 100 g/4 oz butter, 175 g/6 oz soft brown sugar, 2 eggs, 225 g/8 oz wholemeal self-raising flour 1 × 5 ml sppon/1 tsp each baking powder, mixed spice, ground cinnamon and 3 × 15 ml/3 tbsp milk. Process for 10–20 seconds to mix wet and dry ingredients. Add extra milk if the mixture is too stiff. Return the apples to the processor and pulse to mix. Spoon into the prepared tin and sprinkle the top with demerara sugar and a dusting of cinnamon. Bake at 170°C/325°F/gas 3 for 1½ hours or until firm to touch. Turn out and cool on a wire rack.

Apple Sauce

Using the double bladed knife, roughly chop 450 g/1 lb peeled and cored cooking apples, cook with 50 g/2 oz sugar until soft. Cool slightly, then process for 5 seconds until smooth. Flavour with cinnamon and/or nutmeg if desired.

Normandy Tart

Make 175 g/6 oz rich Shortcrust Pastry (page 87), use to line a 23 cm/9 in flan tin; chill. Flavour 1 quantity Apple Sauce, (above) with 2 egg yolks 1 × 15 ml spoon/1 tbsp Calvados or brandy, process for 10 seconds until smooth. Prick the pastry base all over and bake blind at 200°C/400°C/gas 6 for 10–12 minutes until firm. Spread the apple sauce over the base. Using the slicing disc, slice 3 large peeled and cored eating apples, such as Granny Smith's, and arrange in concentric rings on top of the sauce. Dust lightly with soft brown sugar. Reduce oven temperature to 190°C/375°F/gas 5 and cook for 30 minutes, or until apples are tender. Brush with warmed apricot jam while still warm to glaze.

Apple Scones

Make 1 quantity Scone recipe (page 106), mix in 1 coarsely grated small cooking apple and ½ tsp cinnamon. Proceed as for basic recipe.

See also Mincemeat.

APRICOTS

Double bladed knife

Dried: Dried apricots can be pureed or chopped (page 44) for use in cakes, desserts and preserves using the double bladed knife.

Fresh: Fresh apricots can be pureed (page 97) before or after cooking.

AUBERGINE

Slicing Disc

Slicing: Cut aubergine into quarters lengthwise to fit the feed tube, then slice, pressing down with a moderate pressure with the pusher.

Aubergines Parmigiana

Thickly slice 2 medium-sized aubergines, sprinkle with salt and leave for 30 minutes. Rinse well and dry thoroughly. Meanwhile, using the double bladed knife and the motor running, drop two cloves of garlic through the feeder tube. Turn off the machine and add 1 small quartered onion, process until chopped. Fry in olive oil until soft. Stir in 225 g/8 oz chopped canned tomatoes and season with plenty of black pepper. In a separate pan, fry the aubergine slices in olive oil until golden brown and drain on absorbent paper. Arrange the slices in an ovenproof shallow dish. Place 100 g/4 oz prosciutto or ham on top of the aubergine and top with the tomato sauce. Sprinkle 50 g/2 oz grated Parmesan cheese over the top and dot with a little butter. Bake at 180°C/350°F/gas 4 for 30 minutes until golden.

AVOCADO

Slicing disc
Double bladed knife

Slicing: It is possible to slice avocado in the processor but select fruits that are not too soft or you will have problems removing the slices from the bowl. Peel the avocado cut in half, discard the stone, then cut again to fit the feeder tube. Slice thickly, pressing down gently to avoid damage. Sprinkle with lemon juice to avoid discolouration.

Puree: Use the double bladed knife to puree peeled and stoned avocados for soups, dips and sauces.

Guacamole

Fit the double bladed knife and add ½ green pepper; process for 3 seconds, then add 2 spring onions cut in 2.5 cm/1 inch pieces, 2 large peeled and quartered tomatoes; process for a further 5 seconds. Add the flesh of 1 large or 2 small ripe avocados, juice of ½ lemon or 1 lime, few drops Tabasco sauce and salt and pepper to taste. Process for 5 seconds, scrape the mixture down the sides of the bowl and continue to process for another 5–8 seconds; do not over-process. Chill.

B

BABY FOOD

Double bladed knife

The food processor purees food so fine that it is suitable for the very youngest baby. The only drawback is that the conventional processor does not cope with very small quantities very easily, although several manufacturer's do now have a mini-bowl attached to the machine which does process small quantities. Most of these small bowls do process the food finer than their larger counterparts so are particularly well suited to making baby foods. Most of these machines do not have sealed lids so are unsuitable for processing liquids or very fluid purees except in very small quantities. There are also very small processors on the market that are designed to meet the needs of a tiny child.

Process 450 g/1 lb apples or carrots at a time and freeze in ice-cube tray. When frozen transfer to plastic bags and label. As the baby grows and becomes able to take slightly textured food use the pulse method to control the processor to leave very small pieces in the food. These pieces can become bigger as the baby grows.

Remember when processing baby foods that hygiene is more important than ever. Always check that the processor and blade are really clean.

BANANA

Slicing disc
Double bladed knife

Slicing: Cut the ends off a firm banana to make the slices straight, and cut in half. Place vertically in the feeder tube side-by-side. Slice using a gentle pressure on the pusher. Sprinkle lemon juice over the slices as soon as possible to prevent discolouration.

Puree: For recipes that require pureed or mashed banana, such as milk shakes, banana breads or cakes or banana souffles, use the double bladed knife and add 1 × 15 ml spoon/1 tbsp lemon juice.

Tip

Because the banana is a curved shape some of the banana slices may be oblong rather than round. To minimize this effect very gently rub the banana with hands to straighten as much as possible without splitting.

See Milk Shakes.

BASIL

See Herbs · Pesto

BATTER

Double bladed knife

Lump-free batters for pancakes, Yorkshire puddings, etc. can be made in seconds simply by mixing all the ingredients together in the bowl with the double bladed knife fitted. Do not have the pusher in the feed tube.

Pancakes and Yorkshire puddings: Process together, until smooth 100 g/4 oz plain flour, a pinch of salt, 300 ml/½ pint milk and 1 egg. Leave to stand for 30 minutes.

Coating batter for fritters, fish or vegetables: Use 100 g/4 oz plain flour, a pinch of salt, 1 egg and only 50–75 ml/2–3 fl oz milk. Add a generous pinch of bicarbonate of soda, if desired.

BECHAMEL SAUCE

Double bladed knife

Basic white sauce is one of the cornerstones of cookery. Using the processor, lump free sauce is easily achieved every time; do not be put off by the strange texture of the uncooked mixture as it rapidly becomes smooth as the milk heats and the sauce begins to thicken.

Place 25 g/1 oz chopped butter, in the bowl with 300 ml/½ pint milk and 1½ × 15 ml spoons/1 tbsp plain flour for a pouring sauce, 2 × 15 ml spoons/2 tbsp flour for a thicker sauce. Process for 20 seconds until smooth. Pour into a pan (preferably non-stick) and cook over a moderate heat, stirring constantly with a wooden spoon until thickened.

Cheese Sauce: Add 100 g/4 oz grated cheese (page 31) to the cooked sauce, plus a generous pinch nutmeg or mustard.

Parsley Sauce: Chop 5 × 15 ml spoons/5 tbsp fresh parsley first for 5 seconds then add the ingredients as usual.

Mushroom: Chop 100 g/4 oz cooked mushrooms (page 78), add to the cooked sauce and continue cooking for a further 2 minutes.

Tip

A lumpy sauce can be rectified by processing for a few seconds in a food processor.

BEARNAISE SAUCE

Double bladed knife

The classic French sauce is served with red meats, most usually with steak. However, it is also good with economical dishes such as meatloaf. Using the double bladed knife chop a small onion very finely then transfer to a small saucepan. Add 2 × 15 ml spoons/2 tbps wine vinegar, bring to the boil and continue to cook until the liquid is reduced by half. Meanwhile, process 1 whole egg, 1 egg yolk and ½ × 5 ml spoon/½ tsp Dijon mustard for 5 seconds. With the motor running, slowly pour 100 g/4 oz melted unsalted butter through the feeder tube. Add to the sauce pan and stir with a wooden spoon to mix. Use as soon as possible.

BEEF

See Meat.

BEAT

Double bladed knife

Culinary term used to describe mixing ingredients together quite quickly and with some force to both blend them together and to add air to the mixture. Traditionally this is done with a wooden spoon but in the food processor the double bladed knife is used. The pusher should not be in the feeder tube.

BISCUIT-BASE

Double bladed knife

Using the double bladed knife, process 175 g/6 oz digestive biscuits for 15–20 seconds until crumbed. Pour in 75 g/3 oz melted butter and up to 50 g/2 oz demerara sugar, if liked. Process for about 5 seconds to mix. Press into a 20 cm/8 in loose-bottomed cake tin. If the case is not baked after filling, bake at 160°C/325°F/gas 3 for 10 minutes, then leave to cool.

BISCUITS

Double bladed knife

The processor can make many biscuit recipes in a few seconds. For those that use the creaming or all-in-one method, see page 27; for those that are rubbed-in, see page 28. Ingredients such as raisins, chocolate chips or oats should be added after the mixture has been processed so they do not lose their texture or characteristic shape.

Crunchy Oat Biscuits

Place 100 g/4 oz margarine, 125 g/2 oz soft brown sugar, 1 egg, 100 g/4 oz self-raising flour, 2 × 5 ml spoons/2 tsp milk in the bowl and process for 20–30 seconds until the ingredients are mixed. Scrape down the sides of the bowl and add 50 g/2 oz each of desiccated coconut and quick-cooking oats and process for about 3–5 seconds to blend. Do not over-process or the mixture will loose its texture. Drop spoonfuls onto a lightly greased baking sheet and cook for 7–10 minutes at 180°C/350°F/gas 4. Cool on a wire rack.

BLEND

Double bladed knife

To blend is the culinary term that means to mix two or more ingredients together, usually until smooth. In the USA, and sometimes in Britain, the term means to use a blender/liquidiser. The food processor can perform both types of blending using the double bladed knife.

Tip
If your machine has variable speed control, use a low speed to blend liquids.

BREAD

Double bladed knife
Plastic knife

Bread dough is made so quickly and easily in the food processor as the time required to knead the dough adequately is reduced to only one minute. Furthermore, the texture of the bread is reliably even. A basic recipe is given, but the same process may be followed for most bread or yeast-based cake recipes. Some machines are able to process two or even three times the quantities given here, so check the manufacturer's handbook for capacity.

Tip
Combine technology, make the dough in the processor, then place the bread to rise in the microwave. Heat for 10 seconds on HIGH and leave for 5–10 minutes, then repeat until the dough has risen to twice its original size. This cuts rising time by one half.

Place 375 g/12 oz strong white flour and 1 ×5 ml spoon/1 tsp salt in the bowl fitted with the dough blade or the double sided knife and process for 3 seconds. Dissolve 1 × 5 ml spoon/1 tsp dried yeast and 1 × 15 ml/ 1 tbsp each of cooking oil and sugar in 240 ml/8 fl oz lukewarm water. With the motor running, gradually add the liquid through the feeder tube, then, once the dough is formed process for 1 minute. Leave to rise in an oiled plastic bag in a warm place until doubled in bulk. Punch down the dough then return to the processor and process for another 45 seconds. Shape into a circle about 15 cm/6 in diameter and place on an oiled baking sheet. Leave in a warm place, covered in oiled plastic until double in size – 30–45 minutes. Bake in a preheated oven at 190°C/375°F/gas 5 for about 30 minutes until golden and hollow sounding when tapped on the bottom.

See Knead; Yeast Doughs.

BREADCRUMBS

Double bladed knife

Dried Breadcrumbs: Use bread that has been dried in a low oven. The crusts can be included. Use as a topping, in rissoles or meat loaves or as a coating for fried foods.

Fresh: For 100 g/4 oz breadcrumbs, tear into pieces about 6 slices of bread with the crusts removed and place in the bowl. Process until crumbs of the correct texture are produced.

Tip

Make breadcrumbs from bread which has become stale or French bread that has been warmed but not eaten. Freeze the crumbs in plastic bags until required.

BUTTER

Double bladed knife

Savoury Butters: Butters flavoured with herbs or spices can be used to add interest to simply-cooked steak, chops, fish or vegetables. They can also be spread on French bread or used as a base for canapes. If flavouring with chopped herbs, process these in the bowl before adding the butter.

Devilled Butter: Add 100 g/4 oz chopped unsalted butter to the food processor bowl fitted with a double bladed knife. Process until soft, then add 5 ml spoon/1 tsp prepared English mustard, 2 × 5 ml spoons/2 tsp each vinegar and Worcestershire sauce, 5 ml spoon/1 tsp tomato puree, 2 egg yolks and salt and cayenne pepper to taste; pulse to mix.

Lemon Butter: Add 2 × 5 ml spoons/2 tsp each grated lemon rind and lemon juice to 100 g/4 oz softened butter. Season to taste.

Sweet Butters: Used to top pancakes, waffles or crumpets, use unsalted butter flavoured with maple or golden syrup, brown sugar and cinnamon or honey.

Sweet Lemon Butter: Add 2 × 15 ml spoons/2 tbsp icing sugar and 2 × 5 ml spoons/2 tsp each lemon rind and juice to 100 g/4 oz butter in the bowl. Process until evenly mixed.

Hard Sauce or Brandy Butter: To 100 g/4 oz softened butter add 2 × 15 ml spoons/2 tbsp brandy, 25–50 g/1–2 oz icing sugar and the rind of ½ lemon.

At least one manufacturer has a special paddle attachment that makes fresh butter from whipping cream in 4–5 minutes.

C

CABBAGE

Coleslaw disc
Slicing disc

Cut the cabbage into wedges that are small enough to fit down the feeder and slice, or use the coleslaw disc for a grated effect.

Coleslaw

Fit the double bladed knife and finely chop 1 onion. Fit the coleslaw or slicing disc and take 450 g/1 lb white cabbage and process. Using either the coleslaw or coarse grating disc, grate 250 g/8 oz carrots. Fit the slicing disc and slice 1 green pepper. Combine the vegetables in a bowl and season generously with salt and pepper. Mix 1 × 15 ml spoon/1 tbsp dry mustard with a little white wine vinegar until smooth, then make up to 150 ml/5 fl oz with more vinegar. Pour over the vegetables, cover and marinade overnight. The following day, strain off as much vinegar as possible. Mix the coleslaw with 150 ml/5 fl oz mayonnaise (see page 70).

CAKES

Double bladed knife
Plastic blade
Whisk attachment

Creamed, all-in-one and pouring method cake mixtures are very successfully made in the standard food processor. Do not have the pusher in the feeder tube. Be careful not to over-process creamed or all-in-one method mixtures or the mixture will go runny and the resulting cake will be dry. Add ingredients such as dried fruit, nuts and dessicated coconut after the basic mixture has been processed so they maintain their texture.

For fatless sponge cakes a whisk attachment is necessary. The initial processing time is quite long, 6–8 minutes, as it takes time for sufficient air to be incorporated into the mixture so that the whisk leaves a definite trail mark that takes at least 10 seconds to sink into the mixture.

Tip
Recipes not written specially for the food processor may require less liquids than when conventionally made. Add three-quarters of the specified amount adding the remaining liquids only if required.

Victoria Spong Cake (all-in-one method)
In the bowl place 150 g/6 oz each of butter or margarine (cut into small pieces), caster sugar and self-raising flour, 1 × 5 ml spoon/1 tsp baking powder and 3 eggs. Process for 15 seconds then scrape down the sides of the bowl. Process for a further 10–15 seconds until well blended.

Divide the mixture between two 18 cm/7 in greased and bottom-lined sandwich tins and bake at 180°C/350°F/gas 4 for 20–25 minutes until golden and firm to touch. Cool on a wire rack, then sandwich together with jam and optionally, whipped cream, and dust the top with icing sugar.

Swiss Roll
With the whisk attachment fitted, whisk together 3 eggs and 75 g/3 oz caster sugar until the mixture has doubled in volume and the whisk leaves a definite trail mark – 6–8 minutes. Add the flour, pulsing until just incor-

porated. Pour into a greased and lined 30 × 20 cm/ 12 × 8 in Swiss roll tin and bake at 200°C/400°F/gas 6 for 10–12 minutes until golden brown. Turn out onto a sheet of greaseproof paper sprinkled with caster sugar and cut off the crisp outer edges of the cake. Spread with warmed jam and roll up. Leave to cool on a wire rack.

Light Fruit Cake

Cream together 100 g/4 oz diced butter and 100 g/4 oz caster or soft brown sugar until light and fluffy, 20–30 seconds depending on temperature of the butter; scrape down the sides of the bowl once during processing. Lightly beat 2 eggs with a fork and, with the motor running drizzle down the feeder tube until almost incorporated. Add 150 g/5 oz flour and 25 g/1 oz ground almonds and process using the on–off method scraping down the sides of the bowl if necessary. Add 100 g/4 oz mixed dried fruit and 1 × 15 ml spoon/1 tbsp milk and 1 × 5 ml spoon/1 tsp mixed spice and process using the on-off method to blend without chopping the fruit. Turn into a greased and lined 18 cm/7 in round deep tin and bake at 160°C/325°F/gas 3 for about 1 hour or until a skewer inserted into the centre comes out clean. Cool for 5 minutes then turn out onto a wire rack.

CAKE CRUMBS

Double bladed knife

Place leftover cake in the processor fitted with the double bladed knife and process for 10–15 seconds for 225 g/8 oz cake. Use in truffles, treacle tarts etc.

CARROTS

Slicing disc
Grating disc
Shredding disc
Double bladed knife

Chopping: Cut carrots into even-sized pieces and process until evenly chopped.

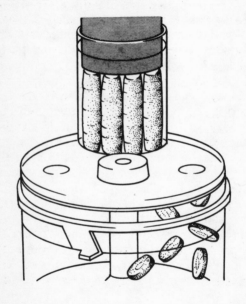

Slicing, grating or shredding: Position in the feeder tube, several peeled, topped and tailed carrots cut to the same length as the feeder tube. With the slicing, grater or shredding disc in place, process the carrots using a moderate pressure on the pusher. If longer pieces of grated or shredded carrot are rquired, cut the carrots to the same length as the feeder tube and place horizontally in the tube, stacking several pieces in position and process using a firm pressure on the pusher.

Puree: Cut the carrots into even-sized pieces and cook until tender. Process using the double bladed knife until smooth, adding cooking liquid, milk or cream through the feeder tube as desired.

CAPACITY

This is the amount of mixture the food processor can handle at one time. Domestic models range from around a 1–3.7 litre bowl. The capacity is also limited by the motor size. Some models can handle 1.35 kg/3 lb pastry or bread dough while others can only process 450 g/1 lb. It is important not to exceed the capacity of the processor as this could cause the mixture to ooze out of the lid of the machine or put undue stress on the motor, causing it to cut out. Check manufacturer's handbook for details.

CELERY

Slicing disc

Slicing: Remove strings from celery and cut into lengths to fit the feeder tube. With the slicing disc in position, fit several pieces of celery in the feeder tube and process using a moderate pressure on the pusher.

CHEESE

Slicing disc
Grating disc
Double bladed knife

Grating: For most dishes it is quicker and easier to use the double bladed knife to finely chop cheese where the recipe states 'grated cheese', especially if the processor fitted with the same blade is used for other tasks in the preparation of a dish. 225 g/8 oz Cheddar cheese can be finely chopped in this way in 25–30 seconds. Perfect evenly grated cheese, however, is obtainable in roughly the same amount of time using the grating disc attachment. Use only hard or semi-hard cheeses, and most are best processed chilled.

Parmesan cheese can be grated using the double bladed knife. Have the cheese at room temperature and, with the motor running, drop 2.5 cm/1 in cubes of cheese down the feeder tube. Continue to process until the desired texture is achieved. Process a large piece of cheese so it is always at hand and keep in an airtight container in the refrigerator or freezer until required. Some manufacturer' make a separate Parmesan cheese grating accessory.

Tip
Small pieces of leftover cheese can be grated for chopped and stored in an airtight container for use on soups, pizzas or in sauces.

Slicing: Semi-hard cheese is sliced when chilled using the slicing disc. Cut into large pieces to fit the feeder tube and process with a moderate pressure on the pusher. Ideal for sandwiches, cheese on toast or baked dishes, such as pizza.

Soft Cheeses: Can be softened for easy mixing in pâtés, sauces and desserts by processing for a few seconds with the double bladed knife. Cottage cheese can be 'sieved' for use in cheesecakes etc. by processing with the double bladed knife for a few seconds, scraping the bowl once.

Cheesy Supper Bake

With the double bladed knife fitted, place 1 small quartered onion, 6 medium slices wholemeal bread, 100 g/4 oz cheese, cut into 4 pieces and a few heads of parsley in the bowl, process for 20–30 seconds until the bread is crumbed and the cheese finely chopped. Add 2 eggs, 2 tsp wholegrain mustard, 450 ml/¾ pint milk and process for a further 10–12 seconds until mixed. Pour into a greased baking dish and cook at 180°C/350°F/gas 4 for 35–40 minutes until set and golden on top.

Manhattan Cheesecake

Make a biscuit base (see page 22); do not bake. For the filling, beat 4 eggs for 60 seconds until light. With the motor still running, gradually add 100 g/4 oz caster sugar and 2 × 15 ml spoons/2 tbsp plain flour. Add juice and grated rind of 1 lemon, 5 ml spoon/1 tsp vanilla flavouring, 150 ml/5 fl oz sour cream and 450 g/1 lb low fat soft cheese. Process for about 15 seconds until combined. Pour into biscuit base. Bake in an oven preheated to 160°C/325°F/gas 3 for 30 minutes, then leave to cool in the oven with the door slightly ajar. Serve decorated with fresh fruit such as strawberries, kiwi fruit or cherries.

CHERRIES

Double bladed knife

Fresh Cherry Puree: See Fruit Puree.
Chopping Glace Cherries: Place cherries in the bowl along with 4 × 15 ml spoons/4 tbsp flour or sugar from the recipe and process to the desired texture, set aside or leave in bowl for an all-in-one recipe. Deduct the quantity of flour or sugar used from the quantity when proceeding with the recipe.

CHESTNUTS

Double bladed knife

Chopping: Peeled roasted chestnuts can be chopped in the processor using the double bladed knife for use in stuffings and nut roasts.

Chestnut Puree: Take about 450 g/1 lb chestnuts and cut a slash in each one. Cook in boiling water for 20–25 minutes, then peel and skin. Process in the food processor until smooth adding a little of the cooking liquid to form a soft textured puree. Food processed chestnut puree is never quite as fine as purchased puree so if it is imperative to achieve a very smooth texture, use canned puree.

CHICKEN

Slicing disc
Double bladed knife

Slicing: Roll boneless chicken breasts or thighs into shapes that will fit the feeder tube and wrap in cling film. Place in the freezer until stiff but not frozen – test with the point of a sharp knife, if it cannot be inserted into the chicken, then it is too hard. Slice the chicken using a moderate pressure on the pusher.

Mincing: Raw or cooked chicken can be minced using the double bladed knife.

CHICKPEAS

Double bladed knife

Chickpeas can be pureed to make excellent dips in the processor. Pureed chickpeas are also the basis of several other Middle Eastern recipes including falafel and a popular tomato and chickpea soup. If you are in a hurry, do not cook the chickpeas from scratch, but use the canned variety. One 400 g/14 oz can would be adequate for the recipe below.

Humus

Soak 225 g/8 oz chickpeas overnight and boil until tender. Drain reserving a little of the cooking water and cool. With the motor running, drop 1 clove of garlic down the feeder tube and process until chopped. Add juice of 1 lemon, 2 × 15 ml spoons/2 tbsp each of olive oil and tahini (sesame seed paste), ½ × 5 ml spoon/½ tsp each of salt, chilli powder and ground cumin. Pulse a couple of times to mix. Add the chickpeas and about 4 × 15 ml spoons/4 tbsp cooking liquid and process until smooth, 15–20 seconds depending on the texture you like. Add a little more water if the humus looks too dry. If you are very fond of the taste of tahini, this may be increased up to 6 × 15 ml spoons/6 tbsp, to taste.

CHOCOLATE

Double bladed knife

Chocolate can be chopped or 'grated' using the double bladed knife, but first make sure the chocolate is cold and hard. Break the chocolate into pieces and process until the desired texture is achieved.

CHOP

Double bladed knife

One of the culinary techniques that the food processor performs well, and quickly. Cut foods into even-sized pieces and place in the bowl fitted with the double bladed knife. Process until desired size pieces are formed. For tighter control over the piece size, use the pulsing technique. Process large quantities in several batches, about 400 g/14 oz is the maximum load for the average machine, or the results will be uneven. If the machine has a variable speed control, use high speeds with hard foods and lower speeds with soft foods such as tomatoes.

Tips

Make sure that the bowl is dry before processing hard foods or dry ingredients or they may stick to the sides of the bowl and fail to be processed further.

Some foods such as hard cheeses and chocolate can be 'grated' using the double bladed knife – i.e. cut very finely suitable for use where a recipe requires grated ingredients. This may be more convenient than fitting the grating disc.

Take care not to overfill the bowl otherwise the food will be unevenly processed.

Where several ingredients have to be chopped, begin with the hardest, partially chop and then add the next ingredient, partially chop and so on until all the ingredients are chopped. Experience will enable you to judge how much processing each food will require.

Think of the blade as a knife, and do not use it to chop anything that is too hard for your favourite chopping knife, such as coffee beans, as this will result in blunting and damaging the blade.

CITRUS PRESS

This resembles a mechanized lemon squeezer. The cone is fitted to the top of the processor then you press the fruit into the cone as it turns. A sieve-like base catches the pips and the bits of flesh that come off the fruit so that the juice is clear. Some citrus presses have two different cones, one for limes and lemons and one for oranges and grapefruits. If a second cone is not supplied, make a small slit in the centre of the fruit half with a sharp knife so that it will sit comfortably on the cone.

The citrus press is most effective when the fruit is at room temperature or even slightly warmed. Do not use fruit straight from the fridge as the juice yield will be low.

Tip
Warm the fruit before pressing by leaving for a short while in very hot water, or placing in the microwave for 10–12 seconds, depending on the size of the fruit, on HIGH.

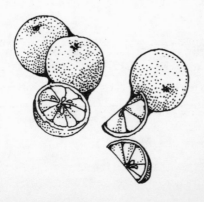

COCONUT

Double bladed knife
Grating a disc

Cut a peeled coconut into 2.5 cm/1 in cubes. Fit the double bladed knife, and, with the motor running, drop the coconut through the feeder tube. Process until the desired texture is achieved.

For grated coconut, cut into wedges to fit the feeder tube and grate using a moderate pressure on the pusher. The size of the final shredded pieces depend on the grater disc used and the width of the coconut pieces in the feeder tube.

Tip

For making coconut cream for use in curries and oriental desserts, process the coconut with the double bladed knife then add 240 ml/8 fl oz very hot milk down the feeder, process until smooth. Transfer to a bowl and add a further 1 litre/ 1½ pints hot milk. Allow to cool then strain through muslin reserving the liquid.

COFFEE

Do not attempt to grind coffee beans in the food processor.

COURGETTES

Slicing disc
Shredding or thick grating disc

Slicing: Cut the courgettes into lengths to fit the feeder tube and place usually two pieces at a time in the tube.

Process through the slicing disk using a moderate pressure on the pusher.
Grating: Use the shredding disc or thick grating disc.

Courgette Pancakes

Grate 300 g/10 oz courgettes using the grating disc, turn onto a plate and set aside. Lightly beat 2 eggs with the double bladed knife, add 50 g/2 oz plain flour, ¼ × 5 ml spoons/¼ tsp bicarbonate of soda and a pinch of salt. Process for 5 seconds, scrape down the sides of the bowl and process for another 5 seconds. Return the courgettes to the bowl and pulse to mix. Wipe a heavy frying-pan with a piece of absorbent kitchen paper soaked in oil (preferably use a pan kept for pancakes and omlettes). When hot, add about one-quarter of the batter and turn the pan to create a thick circular pancake. Cook until golden on one side, flip and cook the second side. Repeat with the remaining batter. Serve with French bread or with a tomato sauce (page 117) if desired.

COURT BOUILLON

Double bladed knife

This is a basic stock used when poaching fish to provide the flavour that would be lacking if poached in water. Take 450 g/1 lb carrots, 2 medium onions, quartered, 1 stick celery, 4 springs parsley, 2 sprigs thyme, 2 cloves garlic and process for 30–40 seconds until the vegetables are chopped. Place in a saucepan with 2 litres/4 pints water, 150 ml/¼ pint vinegar, 1 bay leaf and 1 × 15 ml spoon/1 tbsp salt. Slowly bring to the boil and simmer for 20 minutes, add 6 peppercorns and cook for another 10 minutes. Strain and use as required.

CREAM

Double bladed knife
Whisking attachment

Cream 'whipped' using the double bladed knife is suitable for topping a trifle or filling a cake but it does not double in volume or hold its shape sufficiently for piping. However, some models do have a whisking attachment which will whip the cream until firm. For good results it is usually necessary to process about 200 ml/7 fl oz cream in one batch. Do not have the pusher in the feeder tube.

Tip
Chill the double bladed knife and the bowl before whipping cream.

CRUDITES

Shredding disc
French fry/chipper disc
Slicing disc

Small sticks of raw vegetables usually served with dips. Try carrots, celery, celeriac, kohl rabi using the shredding disc or French fry disc and red and green peppers with the thick slicing disc.

CRUMBLE MIX

Double bladed knife

Follow the basic recipe for both sweet and savoury crumbles, then flavour to suit the filling.

Place 225 g/8 oz flour in the bowl fitted with the double bladed knife. Add a pinch of salt and work for 5 seconds to sift. Add 100 g/4 oz chopped margarine or butter to the flour and process for about 15 seconds until the mixture resembles breadcrumbs. Add flavourings, if using and process until just mixed.

Sweet Crumbles: Add 100 g/4 oz sugar. The grated rind of 1 lemon, 50 g/2 oz sultanas and/or 25 g/1 oz chopped almonds can be added. The flour can be reduced by 50 g/2 oz and replaced with rolled oats.

Savoury Flavourings: 50 g/2 oz grated cheese plus ¼ × 5 ml spoon/¼ tsp paprika and pinch dry mustard. 50 g/2 oz chopped nuts.

2 × 15 ml spoons/2 tbsp chopped fresh parsley.

Reduce flour by 50 g/2 oz and replace with rolled oats.

CUCUMBER

Slicing disc
Grating disc

Slicing: Thin, even slices of cucumber can be obtained by using the thinnest slicing disc and pressing the cucumber through the feeder with an even pressure on the pusher.

Grating: Use the coarse grater disc.

Cucumber Dip

Peel 1 medium cucumber and grate in the food processor. Combine with 1 crushed clove of garlic, 300 ml/½ pint plain yogurt, 1 × 15 ml/1 tbsp olive oil, 1 × 5 ml/1 tsp white wine vinegar, ½ × 5 ml spoon/ ½ tsp salt and 1 × 5 ml spoon/1 tsp dried dill weed. This is also delicious with lamb kebabs or fried fish.

CUSTARD

Double bladed knife

Lumpy custard will be a thing of the past once this easy version is tried.

Place 1 whole egg plus one egg yolk, ½ × 5 ml spoon/½ tsp vanilla essence in the bowl. Process for about 5 seconds until the egg is lightly beaten. Mix 1 × 15 ml spoon/1 tbsp cornflour with a little milk taken from 300 ml/½ pint. Add to the egg mixture and pulse to mix. Bring the milk to the boil and, with the motor running pour in the milk. Once all the milk is added process for about 5 seconds. Return the custard to the pan and cook over the gentlest heat available, stirring constantly with a wooden spoon until the custard thickens, cook for one minute more and serve hot or cold.

CUTTING-IN

Term used to describe process of rubbing fat and flour together to form a mixture that resembles breadcrumbs used in pastry, cake and biscuit making. It can be done very quickly in the food processor with the double bladed knife fitted. Use fat that is firm, not at room temperature.

D

DATES

See Dried Fruit.

DIPS

Double bladed knife

Dips can be served as informal first course or as an accompaniment to nibbles at a drinks party. The food processor prepares most dips in a matter of seconds.

Tuna Dip

Combine in the food processor, 1 200 g/7 oz can drained tuna fish, 150 ml/5 fl oz sour cream, ½ small red pepper, cut into 2.5 cm/1 in pieces, salt and pepper, dash each Worcestershire sauce and Tobasco sauce to taste. Process until the fish is smooth and the pepper finely chopped. Adjust the seasoning and serve chilled.

Creamy Cashew Dip

Put 75 g/3 oz cashew nuts, ½ clove garlic, 3 × 15 ml spoons/3 tbsp oil and 50 ml/2 fl oz water in the bowl and process until smooth. With the motor running slowly pour 50 ml/2 fl oz oil through the feed tube. Season to taste with salt, pepper and paprika.

See also Cucumber Dip (page 41), Guacamole (page 18), Humus (page 35).

DRESSINGS

Double bladed knife

Although a simple vinaigrette benefits from a quick whiz in the food processor it is often more convenient to give it a shake in a jar. However some of the thicker salad dressings are worth making in the processor.

Blue Cheese Dressing
With the motor running drop a clove of garlic down the feed tube and process until chopped. Add 150 ml/5 fl oz sour cream, 50 g/2 oz chopped Danish blue cheese and process until smooth. Season to taste with salt and pepper.

Sour Cream and Honey Dressing
Combine 150 ml/¼ pint sour cream, 2 × 15 ml spoons/ 2 tbsp milk, 1 × 15 ml spoon/1 tbsp lemon juice, 1 × 5 ml spoon/1 tsp honey and salt and pepper to taste. Process until combined.

Herby Yogurt Dressing
With the motor running drop a clove of garlic down the feed tube and process until chopped. Place a handful of parsley, mint, coriander, watercress or tarragon in the bowl and finely chop with the double bladed knife. Add 150 ml/¼ pint yogurt, 1 × 15 ml spoon/1 tbsp white wine vinegar and a pinch of sugar. Process until combined and add salt and pepper to taste.

See also Mayonnaise.

DRIED FRUIT

Double bladed knife

Chopping: To prevent dried fruit from sticking to the blades whilst chopping, dip the blades in cold water before fitting. When appropriate, e.g. dates, check that the fruits are pitted prior to use. Place in the bowl and process until chopped to the required size. For most cake recipes dried fruit should be added after the other ingredients have been mixed together and the pulse technique used to avoid chopping the fruit.

DUMPLINGS

Double bladed knife

Place 100 g/4 oz plain flour, 1 × 5 ml spoon/1 tsp baking powder, ½ × 5 ml spoon/½ tsp salt and a pinch of nutmeg in the bowl and process for 5 seconds to sift and mix. Add 25 g/1 oz butter and process for 5–10 seconds until the mixture resembles breadcrumbs. Add 4–5 × 15 ml spoons/4–5 tbsp milk through the feeder tube until the mixture is fairly wet, but still manageable. Dampen hands and shape into balls. Place on top of a stew 15 minutes before the end of cooking and cover with a lid.

Variations on the basic recipe should be added after the flour and fat have been combined.

Bacon Dumplings: Add 2 × 15 ml spoons/2 tbsp broken crispy bacon and 1½ × 15 ml spoons/½ tbsp fresh chopped herbs, (parsley, tarragon or mixed herbs are good).

Cheese Dumplings: Add a pinch each of dry mustard and cayenne pepper to the flour and then add 50 g/2 oz finely grated cheese after cutting in the fat.

E

EGGS

Double bladed knife
Whisk attachment

Beating: For beaten whole eggs for omlettes, scrambles and baked dishes, use the double bladed knife and process for about 10 seconds, depending on the number of eggs. Do not over-process or the eggs will be hard when cooked.

Whisking: In the past the number of egg-based dishes that could be made in the food processor was limited by the inability to whisk egg whites. However, the development of an egg whisk attachment has changed this. Now souffles, mousses, cakes and desserts using whisked egg whites can be added to the repertoire.

Tip
Whisking the egg whites is often one of the latter stages in a conventional recipe; if using a food processor it is best to whisk the egg whites first and transfer to a bowl. It does not matter if the processor bowl has traces of egg white remaining in it when beating together other ingredients, so there is no need to wash the bowl between processes. The reverse is not true as egg whites will not whisk if they come into contact with traces of protein from the egg yolks, or fat.

Fit the whisk attachment and add the egg whites to the clean, dry bowl. Process until the egg whites have doubled in volume and are standing in firm peaks. Do not over-whisk or the eggs become grainy.

For the best results it is usually necessary to whisk 3 egg whites at one time in a large bowl although some machines have a smaller bowl that will process only 2 egg whites.

Hard-boiled Eggs: Whole hard-boiled eggs, egg whites, and egg yolks can be chopped for use in salads, pies, and for garnishing. Cut the eggs in half and place in the bowl fitted with the double bladed knife. Process until the desired texture is achieved, using the pulsing technique for finer control.

Egg Salad
Finely chop 2 spring onions, 1 stick of celery and 1 carrot in the food processor using the double bladed knife. Add 2 halved hard-boiled eggs and a heaped tablespoon of mayonnaise. Process using the pulsing technique until the egg is roughly chopped and the mixture blended. Use to fill sandwiches or accompanied by a green salad and French bread as a light meal.

Strawberry Souffle
In the food processor, whisk 3 egg whites until stiff, but not dry. Transfer to a clean bowl. Without washing the

bowl, fit the double bladed knife and puree 450 g/1 lb strawberries, flavour with 1 × 15 ml spoon lemon juice, or orange-flavoured liqueur. Set aside. Place 50 g/2 oz each of very soft butter and flour, add 300 ml/½ pint semi-skimmed milk in the bowl; process until smooth. Place the mixture in a heavy pan and cook gently, stirring, until the mixture thickens. Allow to cool slightly, then beat in the egg yolks. (This process can be done by hand in the pan or in the food processor). Stir the strawberry puree into the sauce, then carefully fold in the egg whites (this must be done by hand). Transfer the mixture to a 18 cm/7 in souffle dish and bake for 30–35 minutes at 190°C/375°F/gas 5 until the souffle is firm to touch. Serve with lightly whipped cream (use the double bladed knife for this).

EGG WHISK

See Whisk Attachment.

F

FENNEL

Slicing disc

Slicing: Cut trimmed bulbs into pieces to fit the feeder tube and process using a moderate pressure on the pusher. Use raw in salads, or steam for about 15 minutes and serve with butter and black pepper, or a cheese sauce (page 21).

FISH

Double bladed knife

Minced: Raw and fresh fish can be minced for use in mousses, pâtés and fish cakes. Cut the fish into 2.5 cm/1 in pieces and process using the double bladed knife until the desired texture is achieved.

Two Salmon Mousse

Lightly poach a 225 g/8 oz piece of boneless salmon. Reserve the cooking juices and skin the fish then cut into 2.5 cm/1 in cubes (alternatively use 200 g/7 oz canned salmon, reserving the juices).

Using the egg whisk attachment, stiffly whisk two egg whites then transfer to a bowl, or use a hand whisk. Fit the double bladed knife to the processor, and add 25 g/1 oz each of soft butter and flour along with ½ × 5 ml spoon/½ tsp each of salt, dry mustard, paprika, 1 egg yolk and 150 ml/¼ pint milk. Process for about 10 seconds until the mixture is smooth. Pour into a saucepan and cook over a moderate heat, constantly stirring until the sauce thickens; allow to cool. Place 50 g/2 oz smoked salmon in the bowl, process for 5 seconds, then add the cooked or canned fish and process until smooth. Dissolve 2 × 5 ml spoons/2 tsp gelatine in the reserved salmon juices, adding a little water if required and stir in 3 × 15 ml spoons/3 tbsp lemon juice. Combine with the cooled sauce, then fold in the pureed salmon. Finally fold in the egg whites. Transfer to a lightly greased serving dish or mould and chill for several hours. If turning out the mousse, dip the mould or dish in hot water for 10 seconds before inverting onto a serving plate.

FLOUR

Double bladed knife

Flour can be sifted in the food processor with any other dry ingredients that are required. Place all the ingredients in the bowl fitted with the double bladed knife and process for 3–5 seconds. If not required at the beginning of the recipe, transfer to a bowl or a sheet of greaseproof paper until needed. There is no need to wash the bowl before proceeding with the recipe.

FOOL

Double bladed knife

Make 300 ml/½ pint Fruit Puree (see page 51). Whip 150 ml/¼ pint cream until thick, but not too stiff, and fold into the puree. Sweeten to taste. Alternatively, use half cream and half thick, cold custard. If using custard, beat this into the fruit before folding in cream. To make a low-fat fool, use fromage frais or Greek-style yogurt; for a fluffier texture, fold in one stiffly-whisked egg white.

FRENCH BEANS

Slicing disc

Slicing: Trim the beans to fit into the feeder tube lengthwise and lay as many as possible horizontally in the tube; use a knife to help position beans in place. Process using a moderate pressure on the pusher.

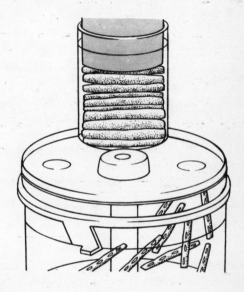

FRITTERS

See batter.

FRUIT

Double bladed knife
Slicing disc

Puree: Fruit purees are quickly made in the food processor, simply place in the bowl fitted with a double bladed knife prepared fruit that is soft, such as fresh apricots, mango, peaches, plums, raspberries, strawberries, or use lightly poached rhubarb or gooseberries and process until smooth. Add caster sugar or honey and lemon juice to taste. Purees made from berries or currants should be passed through a nylon sieve to remove the seeds and pips. Use as a sauce, topping for cheesecakes or as the basis for fruit fools, ice-creams and sorbets.

450 g/1 lb prepared fruit yields about 300 ml/½ pint fruit puree.

Tip
If making fruit puree from frozen fruit, thaw completely and drain thoroughly to avoid a thin puree. Canned fruit should also be drained. The final product should be the consistency of semolina pudding.

Slicing: Many fruits can be sliced using the medium slicing disc. Choose ripe, but firm fruits as soft fruit will squash rather than slice. Apples, pears, peaches, kiwi fruits, bananas and pineapples should be cut to fit the feeder tube and sliced, using just enough pressure to pass the fruit through. Feed a little lemon juice down the tube from time to time to prevent fruits browning. If slicing fruit that is soft such as figs, mango, melon or strawberries use the medium slicing disc.

G

GARLIC

Double bladed knife

Chopping: Garlic is processed before other ingredients are added to the bowl when preparing vegetables for stews, sauces or soups. With the motor running, drop the cloves of garlic through the feeder tube into a clean, dry bowl; they will be chopped as they bounce off the blades.

Garlic bread

Process two cloves of garlic as directed above. Add 50 g/2 oz diced butter (preferably at room temperature). Process until smooth. Cut slashes into the top of a French loaf and place a little of the garlic butter on the exposed bread. Wrap in foil and warm in the oven. Serve with soups, salads and hearty casseroles.

Tip
To add a hint of garlic to dishes such as salad dressings, sauces or vegetable dishes, rub the work bowl with a crushed clove of garlic, before beginning the recipe.

GINGER

Double bladed knife
Slicing disc

Chopping: Peel and cut fresh ginger root into pieces no larger than 2.5 cm/1 in, then, with the motor running, drop down the feed tube into a clean, dry bowl.

Continue to process until the ginger is chopped. To chop crystallized ginger, include about 50 g/2 oz sugar from the recipe to the ginger and process in the bowl until chopped to required size.

Slicing: If the slicing disc turns clockwise, place the ginger against the left side of the feeder tube, and hold in position by using pressure on the pusher or by using a holding tool, if one is provided. The force of the slicing disc rotating should help to hold the food in place. Do not under any circumstances try to guide the ginger in place with your fingers.

Ginger Marinade

Chop a 2.5 cm/1 in piece of ginger and add 2 × 15 ml spoons/2 tbsp each soy sauce, dry sherry and sunflower or soya oil. Process for 3 seconds to mix. Use over Chinese-style fish or shell fish, chicken, pork or beef stir-fry dishes.

GRATE

Cookery term synonymous with shred, the preferred term in the USA. See Grating Disc.

GRATING DISC

Grating or shredding discs vary according to the make and model of the processor, so check manufacturer's specifications for details. Usually the range includes 2, 4 and 6 mm graters and sometimes a special Parmesan or Julienne grater as well.

General guidelines for using the grating disc:

☆ Most foods grate best chilled, this applies to fruit, vegetables and cheeses apart from very hard cheese such as Parmesan. Do not grate frozen items or the disc may be damaged.

* Fruit and vegetables should be ripe but still firm.
* For long shreds position foods horizontally in the feeder tube, for short shreds position them vertically.
* For ease of grating, cut a slice off the bottom of foods such as carrots, so that a there is a flat edge to begin grating from.
* Most manufacturer's advise against grating cooked or raw meats.
* When grating single items position at the left-hand side of the feed tube, if the machine turns clockwise and the right-hand side of the tube for anticlockwise movement, this way the force of the processing will stabilize the food. Use a holding tool, if provided; under no circumstances hold food with the fingers.

GRINDING

Cookery term meaning to process hard foods to a powder. Normally, this can be done in the food processor using the double bladed knife, but very hard or small foods, such as coffee beans and some spices are unsuitable.

H

HAM

See Meat.

HAMBURGER

See Meat.

HARD SAUCE

See Butter.

HAZELNUTS

See Nuts.

HERBS

Double bladed knife

To chop fresh herbs, discard the stalks and place the leaves in the bowl fitted with a double bladed knife. Process briefly until chopped. Fleshy herbs such as basil, mint and sage become very moist on processing so extra care is needed to prevent over-chopping.

Process the entire bunch of herbs at one time as they can be frozen until required. Always have fresh herbs handy in one tablespoon helpings, by mixing with a little water and freezing in ice-cube trays; once frozen store in polythene bags. Alternatively, freeze in the polythene bag and once frozen crush with a rolling pin or mallet to separate. Chopped herbs can also be dried and stored in an airtight container in a dark place.

Tip

Most herbs will process best if they are dry. Wash and allow to dry before use.

HOLLANDAISE SAUCE

Double bladed knife

A tricky and slow sauce to make traditionally, in the food processor it can be made in about one eighth of the time.

In the bowl fitted with the double bladed knife, place one whole egg, 1 × 5 ml spoon/1 tsp lemon juice and a pinch each of salt and white pepper. Process for 5–10 seconds until well blended. With the motor running, slowly pour in 100 g/4 oz hot melted unsalted butter through the feeder tube until all is amalgamated. Serve immediately, or if the sauce has to be kept, place over a pan of hot, not boiling water for up to 20 minutes. Use with fish or with special vegetables such as asparagus as an elegant starter.

Sauce Maltaise

This is a delicate Hollandaise Sauce with a teaspoon of blood orange juice in place of the lemon juice.

HORSERADISH

Double bladed knife

Horseradish Sauce

Peel 1 5 cm/2 in piece horseradish root and cut into cubes about 2.5 cm/1 in. Using the double bladed knife process until finely chopped. Add 4 × 15 ml spoons/ 4 tbsp cider vinegar or lemon juice, 1 × 5 ml spoon/ 1 tsp soft brown sugar, a pinch of salt, ½ × 5 ml spoon/½ tsp dry mustard and 2–3 × 15 ml spoons/ 2–3 tbsp sour cream, cream or plain yoghurt. Process until combined. Use as an accompaniment to roast beef, in sandwiches or in creamy salad dressings.

I

ICE

Double bladed knife

To crush ice, with the motor running and the double bladed knife fitted, drop 1 ice cube down the feeder tube at a time. It makes a lot of noise and the machine should not be near the edge of the work surface as it does move about while crushing the ice.

ICE-CREAM

Double bladed knife

Rich Vanilla Ice-cream

Make 1 quantity of real custard (see page 42), place in a freezer tray and freeze for about 2 hours, until half frozen. Return to the food processor and process for a few seconds, using the pulsing technique, until mushy. Whisk 450 ml/¾ pint whipping cream until thick and fold into the mushy custard. Freeze for at least 4 hours. Place in the refrigerator for 30 minutes before serving.

Quick Peach Ice-cream

Thoroughly drain one 400 g/14 oz can peach halves or stone, peel and quarter 450 g/1 lb fresh peaches. Place in the food processor and add 300 ml/½ pint each of milk and whipping cream, and the grated rind and juice of 1 lemon. Process until smooth. Pour into a freezer try and freeze for about 4 hours until firm. Place in the refrigerator for about 30 minutes before serving.

ICINGS

Double bladed knife

The problem of achieving a lump-free icing without covering the kitchen in a cloud of icing sugar is eliminated when using the food processor for uncooked icings.

Buttercream

Cut 75 g/3 oz unsalted butter at room temperature into pieces and place in bowl with double bladed knife and add 175 g/6 oz icing sugar plus flavourings as required (1–2 × 5 ml spoons/1–2 tsp lemon juice or strong coffee, ½ × 5 ml spoon/½ tsp vanilla essence). Process until smooth. Add a little warm water or milk to thin the buttercream slightly, if required. Sufficient to fill and cover the top of an 18 cm/7 in round cake.

Cream Cheese Frosting

Combine 75 g/3 oz Ricotta or full fat soft cheese, 1½ × 15 ml spoons/1½ tbsp milk, 100 g/4 oz icing sugar, 1 × 5 ml spoon/1 tsp lemon rind, plus either 1 × 5 ml spoon/1 tsp vanilla essence or 1 × 15 ml spoon/1 tbsp rum. Sufficient to fill or cover an 18 cm/7 in round cake.

Fudge Icing

In a small pan, gently heat 75 g/3 oz butter and 250 g/9 oz light brown sugar stirring with a wooden spoon, until the sugar has dissolved. Remove from the heat, cool slightly and pour into the processor fitted with the double bladed knife. Add 1 tbsp milk, ½ tsp vanilla essence. Process until blended. Spread on top and sides of a 20 cm/18 in cake while still warm.

J

JAM

Double bladed knife
Citrus press

Using a processor reduces the initial preparation time when making jams. Begin by very thinly paring off the lemon or orange rind required in the recipe. Place in the bowl fitted with the double bladed knife and add 4 × 15 ml spoons/4 tbsp sugar from the amount specified in the recipe. Process until the required texture is achieved, set aside. Without cleaning the bowl, use the processor to chop stoned and halved apricots, plums or peaches, rhubarb, pears, apples etc. Finally, use the citrus press to extract the juice from the citrus fruit.

Spicy Peach and Plum Jam

Peel, stone and quarter 750 g/1½ lb each of plums and peaches. Process using the double bladed knife until roughly chopped; divide into two or three batches depending on the capacity of the food processor. Place in a preserving pan with 150 ml/¼ pint water and 2 sachets of spices for mulled wine; cook until the fruit is soft; remove spice sachets. Stir in 1.5 kg/3 lb sugar and heat, stirring frequently until the sugar has dissolved. Grate the rind from 1 lemon and 1 orange and add to the pan, then extract the juice from both fruits; stir into the jam. Bring to the boil and boil rapidly until setting point is reached – between 104–106°C/220–222°F on the sugar thermometer or until a teaspoon of hot jam placed on a chilled saucer and left for a couple of minutes, wrinkles when pushed with the finger.

JUICE EXTRACTOR

This comes as a standard accessory with some processors but with others it is an optional attachment. The juice extractor is used for making juice from fruits and vegetables such as apples, carrots, apricots, pineapples, tomatoes, etc.; generally they cannot extract juice from oranges and lemons – that is the role of a citrus press. The fruit is usually chopped into pieces with the skins intact and placed in the machine. The centrifugal force created by the machine's action then forces the juice from the fruit or vegetables, and this goes through a strainer into the bowl. The waste material is collected in the mesh inside the juicer; this must be removed frequently when processing large quantities. For detailed instructions consult the handbook for your machine.

K

KNEAD

This term is most often associated with the energetic and time-consuming process used when making bread and other yeast-based mixtures. By hand, it usually takes about 10 minutes, using a conventional dough hook about 3 minutes and about 1–2 minutes per loaf in the food processor (check manufacturer's specifications for capacity). Some models have a specific dough blade, although the standard double bladed knife seems to do the job quite adequately. Other machines have a dough hook, the main advantage of which is that it will not chop any dried fruit or nuts which are added to the dough.

The dough blade is also used whenever the term 'knead' is used in conventional recipe instructions, such as when making sugar paste or in some pastries.

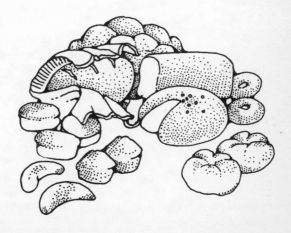

L

LAMB

See Meat.

LASSI

Plastic knife

A cool, refreshing Indian yogurt drink beautifully made in the food processor. Place 150 ml/¼ pint plain yogurt in the processor and process for 5–10 seconds until smooth. With the motor running, pour in 600 ml/1 pint iced water through the feeder tube. Season to taste with salt and pepper and pour into a jug containing ice cubes; garnish with fresh mint leaves.

LEEKS

Slicing blade
Double bladed knife

Slicing: Leeks can be evenly sliced using the widest slicer available. Trim the base and top of the leek and wash very carefully to remove all traces of dirt. Cut lengthwise to fit the feeder tube then place side by side to fill the tube. Process applying a moderate pressure on the pusher.

Puree: Cooked leeks may be pureed using the double bladed knife. Cut the leeks into 2.5 cm/1 in lengths. Place in the processor with 2 × 15 ml spoons/2 tbsp single cream, milk or butter, a pinch of salt and nutmeg and salt and freshly ground black pepper to taste. Process until smooth. Reheat in a saucepan over a moderate heat or in the microwave.

LEMONS

Double bladed knife
Slicing disc
Citrus press

Lemons can be sliced or squeezed using the food processor, and the rind can be chopped fine enough to resemble grated rind. Limes and oranges can be treated in the same way as lemons.

Slicing: Select small lemons that will fit the feeder tube or slice in half lengthwise and cut semi-circular slices. Cut a small slice from the base of the lemon to provide an even cutting edge, place lemon in feeder tube, often inserting the lemon from the bottom is easier than inserting from the top especially if the lemon is a tight fit. Position with the flat cut edge on the slicer disc and process using a firm pressure on the presser. For most purposes the lemon is sliced using the thin or medium thickness slicer.

Tip

As lemon juice keeps in the fridge, juice any lemons that you have partially used, keeping the juice in an airtight container in the fridge until required. Similarly, if you require only the juice, prepare the grated rind, place a teaspoon in each division of an ice-cube tray and moisten with a little water. Freeze until firm, then keep in plastic bag until required. Remember when using that the cube also contains sugar.

Juice: Position in citrus juicer and process for a few seconds until all the juice has been extracted.

Grating: Remove the rind using a potato peeler. Place in the processor bowl fitted with the double bladed knife, add 4 × 15 ml spoons/4 tbsp granulated sugar (deduct this quantity of sugar from the original recipe) and process until the required texture is achieved. Use the pulse action to control the fineness of the grating.

Tip
For decorative lemons take a canelle knife (fruit decorator) and score evenly spaced lines down the fruit vertically. When cut the slices have an attractive fluted edge.

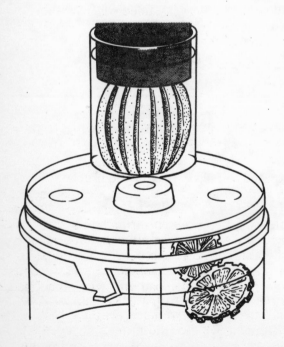

Lemon Sauce Pudding

This is the family favourite which generates a syrupy lemon sauce at the base of a light sponge pudding all by itself.

Whisk 2 egg whites until stiff but not dry and set aside. In the bowl fitted with the double bladed knife place the pared rind of 1 lemon and 25 g/1 oz granulated sugar; process until very fine. Add to the bowl 50 g/2 oz chopped butter, 75 g/3 oz caster sugar, 2 egg yolks, 50 g/2 oz self-raising flour, the grated rind and juice of 1 lemon and 300 ml/½ pint milk. Process for 15 seconds, scrape down the sides of the bowl then process again until smooth, about 15 seconds. Fold into the egg whites and place in a greased ovenproof dish. Place in a roasting tin half filled with hot water and cook for 40–45 minutes at 200°C/400°F/gas 6. Garnish with decorated lemon slices.

LENTILS

Double bladed knife

Lentils can be pureed easily in the food processor using the double bladed knife.

Dhal

Wash 225 oz/8 oz red lentils in several changes of water until the water is clear, then simmer in 600 ml/1 pint fresh water for about 20 minutes until the lentils are tender. Cool slightly, then place the food processor and process for 10 seconds, scrape down the sides of the bowl and process for another 10–15 seconds until smooth. Return to the pan and add 4 chopped fresh tomatoes and season with 1 × 5 ml spoon/1 tsp each of chilli powder and ground coriander and ¼ × 5 ml spoon/¼ tsp each of ground turmeric and salt. Cover and cook over a gentle heat for 10 minutes, then stir in

1 sprig of fresh coriander leaves, chopped. Meanwhile fry a chopped onion in 50 g/2 oz butter or ghee until brown. Sprinkle over the dhal to serve.

LIME

See Lemon.

LIQUIDIZER

Before the advent of food processors, the liquidizer was a standard kitchen aid. It is used to puree wet mixtures such as soups and milk shakes. It's function is now overtaken by the food processor although some models do have a separate liquidizer attachment to overcome the difficulty of processing large quantities of liquid in the processor bowl. The liquidizer does also tend to produce a finer puree than that achieved in the food processor bowl using the double bladed knife.

M

MANGO

The prepared fruit can be pureed for use in ice creams, sorbets, mousses, fools or as a sauce with other fruits.

See Fruit; Sorbets.

MARMALADE

Double bladed knife
Juice extractor

Use the food processor to cut down preparation time. If making Seville-type marmalade remove a thin layer of peel using a potato peeler then place in the bowl and process until the peel is finely cut. If available, use the small bowl fitted to some food processors. The juice can then be extracted from the fruit using the citrus press attachment. If making Dundee-type marmalade where the fruit is boiled whole then the pips removed and the remaining fruit chopped, the chopping can be done using the double bladed knife. Chop 2 or 3 fruits at a time depending on the capacity of the machine.

Dundee Marmalade

Wash 1.3 kg/3 lb Seville oranges very thoroughly. Place in a pan with 3 litres/6 pints water, bring to the boil and simmer for 1½ to 2 hours until the oranges are very soft. Remove the fruit from the pan and cut into quarters. Remove the pips and place in a piece of muslin cloth. Process 8–12 orange quarters until the peel is in very small chucks – about 20–30 seconds depending on the quantity of fruit. Use the pulsing technique to closely monitor the size of the chunks. Return the processed oranges to the pan; repeat until all the oranges are processed. Add 3 kg/6 lb preserving or granulated sugar, 2 × 15 ml spoons/2 tbsp black treacle and the juice of 2 lemons to the pan. Place the lemon pips with the orange pips and tie with string and tie around the pan handles. Heat, stirring until the sugar has dissolved, then bring to the boil and boil rapidly until setting point is reached on the thermometer or a teaspoon of marmalade placed on a chilled saucer will wrinkle when pushed with the finger after about 2 minutes in the fridge. Cool for 10 minutes, then place in sterilized jars and seal.

MARZIPAN

Double bladed knife

Place 250 g/8 oz whole blanched almonds in an oven pre-heated to 150°C/300°F/gas 2 for 10 minutes; cool slightly. Transfer to the bowl and process until smoothly ground. Add 450 g/1 lb sifted icing sugar and process for 2 seconds to mix. Add 2 egg whites and process until the mixture holds together and forms a ball. Do not overwork as the almonds will release too much oil and the paste will be difficult to roll out. If you have a small processor, process in two batches. Sufficient to cover a 15 cm/6 in square, or 18 cm/7 in round cake.

MAYONNAISE

Double bladed knife
or whisk attachment

Foolproof mayonnaise can be made in minutes. With the double bladed knife in position, place in the bowl 2 egg yolks, 1 × 15 ml spoon/1 tbsp lemon juice and a generous pinch dry mustard. Process for 10 seconds. With the machine running, slowly pour 240 ml/8 fl oz olive oil in a steady stream through the feeder tube. After half of the oil has been incorporated the flow may be speeded up a little. Finally add approximately 15 ml spoon/1 tbsp more lemon juice to taste, and season with salt and freshly ground black pepper.

Vinegar may be used in place of lemon juice. Add 1 × 5 ml/1 tsp white wine vinegar with the egg yolks and 2 × 5 ml/2 tsp at the end.

Curry-flavoured Mayonnaise: Add 2 × 5 ml spoons/ 2 tsp curry paste to the finished mayonnaise and process until just mixed.

See also Aioli.

MEAT

Slicing disc
Double bladed knife

Raw meat can be sliced or minced in the food processor while cooked meat can just be chopped. The same techniques apply to beef, lamb and pork as well as to poultry. However, it is essential to ensure that there are no bones – even small ones – in the meat or the processor may be damaged and you will find yourself eating chipped bone in your hamburgers! The bowl and disc or knife must be scrupulously clean and must be washed between processing different types of meat, or other ingredients.

Slicing Raw Meat: Chop the trimmed meat into large pieces to fit the feeder tube and wrap in plastic; freeze until very firm but take care not to over freeze or the slicing disc may be damaged, it should be possible to insert the tip of a sharp knife into the meat before processing otherwise it is too cold. Remove the plastic wrap from the meat and cut into slices using the medium or thick slicing disc; do not attempt to cut meat using the thin disc. The meat should be cut in perfect pieces; if it looks ragged then the meat was not cold enough. Spread the meat out to defrost.

Minced Raw Meat: Trim the visible fast and gristle from the meat and cut into 2.5 cm 1 in chunks. Place about 450 g/1 lb in the food processor at one time and process for 10–15 seconds using the pulsing technique. This is important as meat processed continuously will quickly become pureed. Remove any gristle that has become evident during processing.

Tip

If making meat loaves, balls or rissoles where the meat will be mixed with other ingredients, chop the herbs first then make breadcrumbs (without removing herbs), chop garlic and onions (without removing garlic) then process the meat.

Sliced Cooked Meat: Chill the meat but it should not be necessary to freeze it, as for raw meat, and cut into pieces to fit the feeder tube. Slice using the medium or thick slicing disc and using a moderate pressure on the pusher. This is particularly successful with canned meats such as ham or corned beef although it also works well with leftover roasts. Check there is no bone or gristle in the meat and try to cut the large piece so that the natural line of the meat fibres does not cause the piece to break up, cut across the grain wherever possible.

Cooked Chopped Meat: The procedure is the same as for the raw minced meat and is useful for preparing leftover meat for croquettes, rissoles and meatloaves or for making fillings for sandwiches. It is important to cut the meat into even-sized pieces for best results and to use the pulsing technique to prevent over-processing.

Hamburgers

Process 1 small onion until very finely chopped; set aside. Mince 450 g/1 lb raw lean beef. Return the onion to the bowl and add 3×15 ml spoons/3 tbsp water, 1×5 ml spoon/1 tsp salt and black pepper to taste; process using the pulsing technique to blend. (Worcestershire sauce, chopped parsley, horseradish sauce or a chopped clove of garlic may also be added if desired.) Shape into 4 large or 8 small hamburgers and fry, grill or barbecue until cooked through.

Ham Sandwich Filling
Place 225 g/8 oz cooked ham cut into 2.5 cm/1 in cubes in the processor bowl with 4 spring onions, cut into 2.5 cm/1 in lengths, ¼ green pepper, cut into pieces, 4 gherkins, a dash of Worcestershire sauce and a heaped tablespoon of mayonnaise. Process until the ingredients are finely chopped using the pulsing technique and season with salt and pepper.

MERINGUE
Whisk attachment

With the whisk attachment in position, process 4 egg whites until stiff and able to hold their shape. Add 50 g/2 oz granulated sugar and continue to process for about 1 minute until the mixture becomes glossy, then add 50 g/2 oz caster sugar and process for 15–30 seconds until the sugar is incorporated.

MILK SHAKES
Double bladed knife
or plastic knife
Liquidizer attachment

Use either the double bladed knife or the plastic knife to make milk shakes, unless they contain any hard ingredients, such as nuts or chocolate, when the double bladed knife should be used. Some processors may also include a liquidizer unit or a 'planetary' blade which could be used instead. See manufacturer's instructions for the best method for your model.

Banana Milk Shake
Process together 2 bananas, 2 scoops of vanilla ice cream and 300 ml/½ pint milk.

Chocolate Milk Shake
Process together 2–3 × 15 ml spoons/2–3 tbsp chocolate spread, 300 ml/½ pint milk, 1 scoop chocolate ice-cream and 25 g/1 oz chocolate drops (optional).

MINCEMEAT

Double bladed knife
Grating Disc

Delicious home-made mincemeat requires only a few fruits to be chopped and with the help of the food processor this can be done so quickly.

Finely chop 100 g/4 oz blanched almonds with the double bladed knife; remove from the bowl and chop 225 g/8 oz peeled and cored apples. Grate 1 large carrot using the medium grating disc. Place in a large bowl with 225 g/8 oz each of shredded suet, raisins, sultanas, currants and dark brown sugar. Add 50 g/2 oz chopped mixed peel, 3 × 15 ml/3 tbsp brandy and the juice and rind of 1 lemon. Season with 1 × 5 ml spoon/1 tsp each of cinnamon, nutmeg, ground cloves, and mace. Pack into clean jars, cover and keep for up to 1 month. Tip the jars from time to time to allow the liquid to circulate and keep all the fruit moist.

MINI PROCESSORS

These are generally little food processors that are suitable for handling small quantities of food such as baby's meals, herbs, single portions etc., which a large processor cannot deal with efficiently. These machines usually work with only the equivalent of the double bladed knife and cannot slice or grate.

MINT

Double bladed knife

See Herbs.

MINT SAUCE

Double bladed knife

Place 1 large bunch of mint, about 25 g/1 oz, in the bowl fitted with the double bladed knife along with 2 × 15 ml spoons/2 tbsp granulated sugar and process for 10–15 seconds until finely chopped. Add 1 × 15 ml spoon/ 1 tbsp boiling water and pulse once. Pour in 3–4 × 15 ml spoons/3–4 tbsp white wine or cider vinegar and process for 2–3 minutes.

MOCK WHIPPED CREAM

Plastic knife

This buttery mixture has a texture similar to whipped cream and is a good filling for sponges and pastries.

Sprinkle 1 × 5 ml spoon/1 tsp gelatine over 3 × 15 ml spoons/3 tbsp water in a small bowl. Place over a saucepan of simmering water until dissolved. Place 100 g/4 oz soft butter and 100 g/4 oz caster sugar in the processor bowl fitted with the double bladed knife and process until mixed – 10–15 seconds; scrape down the sides of the bowl. Add a pinch of salt, and a few drops of vanilla essence or the grated rind of ½ lemon and pulse twice to mix, then pour in the dissolved gelatine. Continue to process until the mixture resembles whipped cream, scraping down the sides of the bowl occasionally.

MOUSSE

Double bladed knife
Whisk attachment

Mousses can be made using the double bladed knife only, although the whipped egg whites and cream will not increase in volume nor be as stiff as if an egg whisk attachment is used.

Orange and Lemon Mousse

Sprinkle 1 × 15 ml spoon/1 tbsp gelatine over 4 × 15 ml spoons/4 tbsp water in a small bowl and place over a bowl of simmering water until dissolved. Chill the double bladed knife then fit to the processor and add 2 egg whites. Process for 10 seconds, if the machine has variable speeds, begin the processing slowly. Add a generous pinch of cream of tartar and continue to process until the egg whites hold their shape – approximately 2 minutes. Alternatively, use the egg whisk to whisk the egg whites. Transfer to a bowl. Again using either the double bladed knife or the egg whisk (there is no need to clean bowl or blades), beat 300 ml/½ pint double cream until stiff – 20–30 seconds; transfer to the bowl with the egg whites.

Still without washing the bowl, fit the double bladed knife and process 2 egg yolks and 50 g/2 oz caster sugar until thick. Add the dissolved gelatine, the grated rind and juice of 1 orange and 1 lemon and 1 × 15 ml spoon/1 tbsp orange flavoured liqueur, if liked. Process for 5 seconds to mix. Depending on the capacity of the machine, either return the whisked egg whites and cream to the bowl and process by pulsing 5 times to blend or fold the ingredients together by hand. Transfer to a mould and leave in the refrigerator to set.

See also Two Salmon Mousse, page 49.

MOUSSELINE SAUCE

Double bladed knife
Whisk attachment

Mousseline is the French name for a sauce, most often Hollandaise, that has been lightened by the addition of whipped cream.

Whip 300 ml/½ pint double cream either using a chilled double bladed knife or with the egg whisk, remove and set aside scraping the bowl well. Make Hollandaise Sauce, see page 57. Fold the whipped cream into the completed sauce, and add a few drops of lemon juice if required. Serve with luxurious vegetables such as asparagus.

MUFFINS

Double bladed knife

American-style muffins are made so quickly in the food processor that it is possible to make them for breakfast – well maybe on weekends!

Place 225 g/8 oz flour, 1 × 15 ml spoon/1 tbsp each of caster sugar and baking powder, ½ tsp salt in the bowl and process for 3 seconds to sift. Add 1 lightly beaten egg, 120 ml/4 fl oz milk and 50 g/2 oz melted butter. Process for 5 seconds, scrape down the sides of the bowl and process for a further 2–5 seconds until combined but still slightly lumpy. Flavour with 50 g/2 oz nuts or dried fruit or with a few drops of vanilla essence. Divide between 12 greased muffin or bun tins or paper cases and bake at 200°C/400°F/gas 6 for about 20 minutes until risen and golden brown.

MUSHROOMS

Slicing disc
Double bladed knife

Slicing: Fit the medium slicing disc. For random slices suitable for most general purposes, drop the mushrooms into the feeder tube. If you want perfectly shaped slices, pack the caps in horizontal layers of equal size with each layer facing in the opposite direction to the last. Process using a gentle pressure on the pusher or the mushrooms will become squashed and the slices distorted.

Tip
When preparing mushrooms, simply wipe the mushrooms clean with damp kitchen paper.

Chopping: Fit the double bladed knife and process about 100 g/4 oz of mushrooms at one time to the required texture. If using large mushrooms halve or quarter before chopping. Use the pulsing technique to fine-tune the size of the pieces.

Mushroom Flan

Make 175 g/6 oz Shortcrust Pastry, page 87. Use to line a 20 cm/8 in flan tin and bake 'blind' at 200°C/400°F/gas 6 for about 15 minutes until lightly brown.

Slice 350 g/12 oz mushrooms then set the mushrooms aside. Fit the double bladed knife and chop 1 onion quite finely and cook until soft in 50 g/2 oz butter. Meanwhile, chop 1 hard-boiled egg (page 47) and 3 skinned fresh tomatoes or 3 canned tomatoes (page 116) and set both aside. Add the mushrooms to the onions and cook until they are tender. Using a slotted spoon, transfer the vegetables to the tomato mixture.

Stir 45 g/1½ oz plain flour into the juices in the pan and cook for 1 minute. Gradually stir in 450 ml/¾ pint milk. Cook over a gentle heat until the mixture boils and thickens. Stir in all the vegetables and 1 × 5 ml spoon/1 tsp each of chopped thyme and Worcestershire sauce and salt and black pepper to taste. Pour the filling into the pastry and serve hot or cold.

MUSTARD GLAZE

Double bladed knife

Use as a glaze when preparing roast ham, gammon or pork. Simply baste the meat with the glaze at regular intervals during cooking. Also use as a baste for kebabs or grilled chops.

With the machine running drop 1 clove of garlic through the feeder tube. When chopped drop a 1 cm/½ in piece of peeled fresh root ginger through the tube and chop. Turn off the machine and add 100 g/4 oz Dijon mustard, 2 × 15 ml/2 tbsp spoons light soy sauce, 1 × 15 ml spoon/1 tbsp sunflower or soy oil and ½ × 5 ml spoon/½ tsp each of dried thyme, parsley and salt. Process for 5 seconds to blend, scraping down the sides of the bowl, if necessary. Can be kept in the refrigerator for several weeks.

N

NUTS

Double bladed knife

Chopping nuts by hand is time-consuming and fiddly but in a food processor 100 g/4 oz walnuts can be roughly chopped in just 5 seconds! For most models about 240–375 g/8–12 oz of nuts is the maximum that should be processed at a time. Using the double bladed knife, place the shelled nuts in the bowl and process using the pulsing method until the nuts are processed as required, from roughly chopped through to ground. Take care not to over-process otherwise the nuts will become oily.

Nut Rissoles

Using the double bladed knife, process 1 medium onion and fry in 2 × 15 ml spoons/2 tbsp sunflower oil until soft. Meanwhile, chop 225 g/8 oz mixed nuts (e.g. almonds, cashew nuts, hazelnuts, peanuts and walnuts), 1 large carrot and 4 slices of wholemeal bread until quite fine – if you have a small machine you may have to do this in two batches. Add the onions and 1 × 5 ml spoon/1 tsp each of thyme and parsley. Dissolve 2 × 5 ml spoons/2 tsp yeast extract in 200 ml/7 fl oz vegetable stock and pour down the feeder tube pulsing a couple of times to mix until the mixture is moist but firm enough to handle. Shape the mixture into 8 patties. Dip each into lightly beaten egg and coat in prepared soft breadcrumbs. Shallow fry in sunflower oil for 4–5 minutes on each side. Serve with salads.

Apricot and Brazil Nut Cake

Soak 350 g/12 oz apricots overnight, then drain well. Place 225 g/8 oz Brazil nuts in the processor and chop for 5 seconds until roughly chopped then add the apricots and 100 g/4 oz flaked coconut. Pulse a few times to roughly chop the apricots. Pour 75 g/3 oz melted butter or margarine through the feeder tube. Process for a few seconds to mix. Transfer to a bowl. Without washing the bowl, combine 90 ml/3 fl oz milk and 2 × 5 ml spoons/2 tsp vinegar, 2 eggs, 100 g/4 oz soft brown sugar, 175 g/6 oz plain flour (white or wholemeal) and 1 × 5 ml spoon/1 tsp bicarbonate of soda. Process for 5 seconds, scrape down the sides of the bowl and process for a further 5–10 seconds until smooth. Return the fruit mixture to the bowl and pulse to mix. Bake in a greased and bottom lined 20 cm/8 in ring cake tin and bake at 160°C/325°F/gas 3 for 1 hour or until a skewer inserted into the centre comes out clean.

NUT BUTTER

Double bladed knife

Use the food processor to make your own peanut, almond or cashew butter, then you will know that only the best ingredients have been used.

With the double bladed knife fitted place 350 g/12 oz toasted unsalted nuts in the bowl with 3 × 15 ml spoons/3 tbsp light oil such as safflower or sunflower oil and 1 × 5 ml spoon/1 tsp salt. Process until chunky or smooth according to preference. Add up to 3 × 15 ml spoons/3 tbsp more oil if necessary to form a moist butter. Add a little brown sugar or honey to taste if desired. Store in airtight containers.

O

OMELETTES

Double bladed knife
Whisk attachment

To prepare the eggs for making omelettes, combine 3 eggs, 2 × 15 ml spoons/2 tbsp water, ½ × 5 ml spoon/ ½ tsp salt and a pinch of freshly ground black pepper in the processor bowl fitted with the double bladed knife. Pulse twice to blend the ingredients; if over-blended the omelette will be tough.

Mushroom and Spring Onion Omelette

Slice 50 g/2 oz mushrooms (see page 78) and 2 spring onions (see page 83). Cook gently in 25 g/1 oz butter until soft. Prepare the omelette mixture, add the cooked vegetables and stir quickly. Cook the omelette over a moderate heat until it has just set, then fold in half.

Sweet Souffle Omelette

You need an egg whisk attachment to make this delicious light dessert.

Whisk 3 egg whites until they form stiff peaks either by hand or with the whisk attachment then transfer to a bowl. Insert the double bladed knife, (there is no need to wash the bowl if the whisk attachment has been used) and add the 3 egg yolks, 1 × 15 ml spoon/1 tbsp each of caster sugar and single cream, 2 × 5 ml spoon/2 tsp flour, grated rind of half lemon and a pinch of salt. Process for 5 seconds and scrape down the sides of the bowl, then process for another 5 seconds. Return the egg whites to the bowl and pulse a couple of times until just mixed. Heat 15 g/½ oz butter in a heavy frying-pan and pour in one-quarter of the egg mixture. Fry over a moderate heat for 2–3 minutes until set and golden on one side, flip over and cook the second side. Repeat with the remaining mixture to make 4 small omelettes. Serve with jam or maple syrup.

ON/OFF TECHNIQUE

See Pulsing.

ONIONS

Double bladed knife

Onions may be chopped or sliced in the food processor. Unfortunately processing doesn't prevent watering eyes, but it does at least speed up the business.

Chopping: Peel, then cut into quarters or halves depending on the size of the onions; a large Spanish onion should be cut into at least 8 pieces. With the double bladed knife fitted and using the pulsing technique process onion to the desired texture.

Slicing: Small onions can be used whole but larger ones must be cut in half to fit the feeder tube. Trim a straight edge from the base of the onion and drop into position through the feeder tube. If it is a tight squeeze to insert the onion in at the top, fit into the base of the feeder tube. Use a moderate pressure on the pusher.

French Onion Soup

Slice 675 g/1½ lbs onions and fry gently in 25 g/1 oz butter until the onions are soft and just beginning to brown. Stir in 25 g/1 oz flour and cook for 1 minute. Slowly add 1.2 litres/2 pints good beef stock plus 60 ml/2 fl oz red wine, bring to the boil, stirring constantly. Add 1 × 5 ml spoon/1 tsp dried thyme, 1 bay leaf and salt and pepper to taste. Simmer gently for 30 minutes then stir in 2 × 15 ml spoons/2 tbsp brandy and adjust the seasoning to taste.

ORANGES

Citrus press
Medium slicing disc

Juice: If you like fresh orange juice, then it is definitely worth investing in a citrus press attachment for your machine, if one is not provided, as it juices oranges in seconds and removes the fleshy particles and pips as well. Orange juice keeps well in the fridge for two days and freezes well, so it is worth squeezing a large quantity of oranges at a time and freezing single portions in small plastic bags or containers.

Tip
To gain the maximum yield of juice, warm the oranges in very hot water or place in the microwave for 10 seconds on HIGH.

Slicing: Use the medium cutting disc as the thin slicer makes the oranges difficult to handle. Because of their size, it is usually necessary to cut oranges in half lengthwise; the resulting slices are semi-circular in shape. Also cut a horizontal slice from the base of the orange. Insert the orange into the feeder tube vertically so that it stands on the cut edge (sometimes it is easier to insert them into the feeder tube from the base), and slice using a fairly firm pressure on the pusher. Oranges can also be sliced with the peel and pith removed for use in fruit salads; treat as above but use a lighter pressure on the pusher when slicing.

Orange and Olive Salad
A tangy Italian salad that is delicious with smoked meats or oily fish.

Slice 4 peeled small oranges and arrange on a serving

plate. Slice a small onion into rings (see page 83) and sprinkle over the oranges. Top with 175 g/6 oz large black olives. Combine 4 × 15 ml spoons/4 tbsp olive oil, 1 × 15 ml spoon/1 tbsp lemon juice, a pinch of salt and black pepper and the leaves of 3 large sprigs parsley, process until the parsley is finely chopped.

Orange Protein Cup

Squeeze two oranges using the citrus press, insert the double bladed knife and add 150 ml/¼ pint plain yogurt, 1 egg and a pinch of nutmeg. Process for a few seconds until smooth.

Caramelized Oranges

Slice 6–8 peeled oranges (preferably blood oranges when in season) and arrange in a bowl. Place 4 × 15 ml spoons/4 tbsp each of granulated sugar and water in a small saucepan and heat, stirring, until the sugar has dissolved, then boil without stirring until the mixture is a golden colour; remove from the heat immediately. Add 4 × 15 ml spoons/4 tbsp boiling water and stir until combined while the mixture bubbles furiously. 1 × 15 ml spoon/1 tbsp orange-flavoured liqueur or brandy may be added to the caramel mixture. Allow to cool and pour over the oranges.

P

PANCAKES

See Batter.

PARSLEY

See Herbs.

PASTA DOUGH

Double bladed knife
Plastic blade or Dough hook

In the processor bowl fitted with the double bladed knife or the plastic blade, place 200 g/7 oz plain flour (Italian Durum wheat flour is best but is very difficult to obtain), 2 eggs, 1 × 15 ml spoon/1 tbsp vegetable oil and a generous pinch of salt. Process until the dough is well blended and holds together in one ball. On a lightly-floured surface, roll the pasta out very thinly and cut into thin strips to make tagliatelle or use for filled pastas such as ravioli.

PASTRY

Double bladed knife or
Plastic knife

As the key to success with pastry making is to work the dough as little as possible, pastry made in the food processor is extremely short and light. However, even simple shortcrust pastry does need to be chilled before use otherwise rolling out and transferring the dough to the pie dish will be problematic. Either the double bladed knife or the plastic blade can be used.

Tip
Make up several batches of pastry at one time as uncooked pastry freezes well for up to 6 months.

Shortcrust Pastry

The most versatile type of pastry used for both savoury and sweet dishes. For sweet recipes, it may be flavoured with sugar or vanilla sugar, or with cheese or herbs for savoury ones. For a slightly richer pastry bind with egg yolk in place of water.

Place 185 g/6 oz plain flour in the bowl fitted with the double bladed knife. Add a pinch of salt and work for 5 seconds to sift. Cut into small pieces 85 g/3 oz butter, margarine, white vegetable fat, or a mixture of any two. Add to the flour and process for about 15 seconds until the mixture resembles breadcrumbs. Add 2 × 15 ml spoons/2 tbsp cold water through the feeder tube and process for about 20 seconds until the mixture just binds together. Gather the mixture together kneeding lightly to form a ball of dough. Cover and chill.

Wholemeal Pastry

The high-fibre version of shortcrust pastry.

Instead of plain flour use wholemeal self-raising flour, or 75 g/3 oz wholemeal self-raising flour and 75 g/3 oz white self-raising flour for less heavy pastry.

Tip
When a recipe states an 225 g/8 oz quantity of pastry it means that you should use 225 g/8 oz flour when making the pastry not the weight of the prepared pastry.

Rich Sweet Pastry (Pâté Sucree)

This rich pastry is wonderful for tarts and sweet pies.

With the double bladed knife, place 225 g/8 oz plain, white flour and a pinch of salt in the bowl and process for 5 seconds. Add 175 g/6 oz butter cut into small pieces and process for 10–15 seconds to cut in. Pour in 50 g/2 oz caster sugar and process for a couple of seconds to mix, then bind with 2 egg yolks for 20–30 seconds until the pastry sticks together. Knead the pastry on removing from the processor to form a ball and chill well before use.

Choux Pastry

This type of pastry is used for eclairs, profiteroles, savoury puffs and gougeres; it is the only pastry that is made from a cooked dough. The processor cuts out the arm-breaking beating stage.

Make the dough by heating 150 ml/5 fl oz water in a pan with 50 g/2 oz diced butter until the butter has melted. Bring quickly to the boil. Remove the pan from the heat and stir 65 g/2½ oz flour and a pinch of salt all in one go. Beat with a wooden spoon until the mixture is smooth and forms a ball. Cool slightly and place in the food processor bowl. Switch on the machine and add 2 eggs, one at a time, processing each until incorporated and the mixture is smooth and glossy. Cheese-flavoured choux, add 50 g/2 oz to the finished pastry and process for a few seconds to mix.

Suet Pastry

Place in the processor bowl, 225 g/8 oz plain flour, 100 g/4 oz shredded suet, ¼ tsp salt and 150 ml/5 fl oz water. Process for 15–20 minutes until the mixture binds into a ball. Knead lightly and chill until required.

PÂTÉ

Double bladed knife

These become very quick and easy in the food processor. Some pâtés, such as the chicken liver pâté below are made with cooked meats which are then processed until smooth. Others, often called terrines, are made from uncooked minced meats which are then baked. Using the food processor makes the preparation of either type of pâté very much easier and quicker.

Cheat's Pâté

Incredibly quick to make. Place in the food processor bowl 100 g/4 oz liver sausage and 100 g/4 oz low-fat soft cheese, 1 × 5 ml spoon/1 tsp sherry plus a pinch of dried thyme and black pepper. Process briefly until just evenly combined.

Chicken Liver Pâté

In a small pan, combine 225 g/8 oz chicken livers, 150 ml/¼ pint water, ½ chicken stock cube, 1 whole clove of garlic, 1 small, finely-chopped onion and ¼ × 5 ml spoon/¼ tsp dried thyme. Simmer for 15 minutes, cool slightly and place in the processor fitted with the double bladed knife. Meanwhile, grill 4 rashers streaky bacon until crisp, then crumble into the processor bowl. Add 50 g/2 oz chopped butter and ½ × 5 ml spoon/½ tsp Worcestershire sauce and process until either fairly smooth or very smooth as desired. Place in a bowl and chill for several hours before serving.

PEAS

Double bladed knife

The food processor may be used to make excellent pease pudding.

Pease Pudding

Soak 225 g/8 oz dried peas for at least 4 hours or overnight, drain then boil in fresh water until tender – about 1½ hours; alternatively cover with water and microwave for 10 minutes on HIGH followed by 1 hour on MEDIUM. Meanwhile, chop 1 large onion and 1 large carrot in the food processor fitted with a double bladed knife, and set aside. Drain the peas, reserving some of the cooking liquids, and cool slightly. Place the peas in the food processor fitted with the double bladed knife and add a little of the cooking liquid. Process until smooth, adding more liquid to form a thick but not stiff puree. Return the onion and carrot to the processor with 1 egg, and 1 × 5 ml spoon/1 tsp dried marjoram and salt and pepper to taste; pulse to blend. Measure out 150 ml ¼ pint milk and mix 1 × 15 ml spoon/1 tbsp arrowroot to a paste with a little of the milk, then add the remaining milk and 25 g/1 oz butter. Cook in the microwave on HIGH for 2 minutes, stirring twice, or bring to the boil in a saucepan stirring constantly; simmer until thickened. Pour into the puree and pulse to blend. Place in a lightly greased basin or ring mould, cover and cook on MEDIUM for 12 minutes, or wrap in foil and steam for 1 hour.

PEACHES

See Fruit.

Peach Melba

In a heavy-based saucepan dissolve 100 g/4 oz granulated sugar in 450 ml/¾ pint water, stirring frequently, then bring to the boil and simmer for 5 minutes. Add 4 fresh peaches, peeled, halved and stoned and poach for 5–10 minutes until tender. Remove from the syrup and cool. Place 450 g/1 lb raspberries in the food processor fitted with the double bladed knife and process until smooth. Add 50 g/2 oz icing sugar and pulse to blend. The sauce may then be passed through a sieve, if desired. Put half of the sauce in the base of 4 deep sundae dishes and place the peaches on top, followed by a scoop of vanilla ice cream. Drizzle the remaining sauce over the top.

PEANUTS

See Nuts

PEANUT BUTTER

See Nut Butter.

PEANUT SAUCE

See Satay.

PECAN

See Nuts.

PEPPERS

Slicing disc

Slicing: Very small green, red and yellow peppers can be sliced whole, after removing the core, seeds and white pith, but larger ones will have to be cut in half lengthwise, a slice cut off to form a good cutting edge and processed using a very light pressure. Slice horizontally as vertical slides are not so successful because of their uneven shape. Alternatively, cut off the tops and bottoms of the pepper, make a single lengthwise cut, then roll the pepper to fit the feed tube and process using a light pressure.

Three Pepper Stew

Slice 1 each red, green and yellow pepper. Bash a clove of garlic to split, then wipe it round the inside of a deep frying pan. Add 3 × 15 ml spoons/3 tbsp olive oil and heat. Add the peppers and fry gently for about 5 minutes, turning frequently. Meanwhile, skin 4 large tomatoes and roughly chop using the double bladed knife; pour over the peppers and continue to cook for about 30 minutes until the peppers are tender and the sauce has thickened. Add ½ × 5 ml spoon/½ tsp dried marjoram and salt and pepper to taste.

PESTO

Double bladed knife

This is the classic Italian sauce to accompany pasta made from basil, pine kernels and cheese. Traditionally it is made with a pestle and mortar and takes a long time and a lot of effort to make.

Place 225 g/8 oz fresh basil leaves in the processor with 50 g/2 oz pine kernels, 100 g/4 oz chopped Pecorino or Parmesan cheese. Process for 5 seconds, then with the machine running, drizzle 225 ml/8 fl oz oil through the feed tube. Process for half to one minute until the sauce is perfectly smooth.

This sauce has a pronounced flavour so strong only a little is required at a time; any remaining can be frozen in ice-cube trays until required again.

PINEAPPLE

Slicing disc
Juice extractor

Slicing: Remove the top and base of the fruit and remove the skin. Cut in quarters lengthwise then in half widthwise and remove the central core. The pineapple may now fit the feeder tube, depending on the size of the pineapple, otherwise trim to fit. Process using a medium slicing disc and a moderate pressure on the pusher.

Juice: Peel and cut into pieces following the general guidelines provided by the manufacturer and process in several batches.

PIZZA

Double bladed knife
Slicing disc
Plastic knife

Make 1 quantity Bread (page 24) but instead of forming into a loaf, shape into a circle and place on a pizza plate or baking sheet. While the dough is rising prepare the topping.

With the machine running, and the double bladed knife fitted, drop 12 g/½ oz Parmesan cheese through the feed tube and process until grated; remove and set aside. Insert the slicing disc and slice 1 large green pepper (see page 91) and 50 g/2 oz mushrooms and 100 g/4 oz salami-type sausage (optional), (see page 105). Remove from the bowl and set aside. Slice 1 chilled Mozzarella cheese, cut in half, if necessary; set aside. Fit the double bladed knife and chop either 4 skinned and peeled tomatoes or 4 well-drained canned tomatoes.

Spread the tomatoes over the prepared doughbase and sprinkle with a little oregano and basil and with salt and pepper. Top with the vegetables and sausage and then arrange the Mozzarella on top. Sprinkle with Parmesan cheese; brush a little oil on parts of the base that are exposed. Bake in a preheated oven 220°C/425°F/gas 7 for 15–20 minutes until golden.

PLUMS

See Fruit.

PORK

See Meat.

POTATOES

Slicing discs of a range of thicknesses
double bladed knife
Grating discs
Chipping/French fry disc

The food processor is mainly used in the preparation of raw potatoes. Wash or peel potatoes, remove any 'eyes', bruises and green flesh. The slicing disc can evenly slice potatoes for dishes such as potatoes dauphinois, Lancashire hotpot and moussaka, or even for home-cooked crisps. The grating blade is useful for Swiss rosti, potato pancakes, etc. Use the double bladed knife for roughly chopping potatoes for use in soups and the chipping or French-fry disc for quickly preparing a large quantity of chips.

Do not use the basic food processor for mashing or pureeing cooked potatoes as the result will become sticky (although some manufacturer's have a special press for mashing potatoes). Cooked potato may be quickly mixed with other ingredients in recipes such as potato croquettes when the potato does not have to be smooth. Do not process for more than 15–20 seconds.

Potatoes Dauphinois

Using a medium slicing disc, slice 1 kg/2 lbs potatoes, then using the double bladed knife, finely chop a large onion. Using the fine grater, grate 100 g/4 oz Cheddar or Gruyere cheese. You will also need 150 ml/¼ pint single/light cream or milk and approximately 25 g/1 oz butter. Butter an ovenproof casserole dish and place a layer of overlapping potato slices in the bottom of the dish, dot with butter, sprinkle over some onion and cheese, pour over about one quarter of the cream or milk and season with salt and pepper. Continue the layering until all the ingredients have been used, ending with cheese; pour the remaining cream over the top. Cover the casserole and bake for 1 hour at 190°C/375°F/gas 5 or until the potatoes are soft; remove the lid for the last 15 minutes of cooking. In a microwave cook for 12–15 minutes on HIGH, then leave to stand for 10 minutes before serving.

Swiss Rosti

Boil 675 g/1½ lbs whole potatoes until they are almost tender, drain well, allow to cool then coarsely grate. Season with salt and pepper. Heat 50 g/2 oz butter or margarine in a frying pan (preferably non-stick). Press the potato into the pan and cook over a moderate heat for about 10 minutes until the bottom of the potato cake is golden. Turn the rosti onto a plate, then slide back into the frying pan to cook the second side.

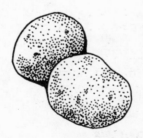

Crisps

Use the thinnest slicing blade to cut 450 g/1 lb potatoes crosswise into slices. Wash well in cold water, drain well and dry with absorbent paper or a cloth. Heat oil in a deep pan to 190°C/375°F, place a small quantity of the crisps in a wire basket and plunge into the hot fat for about 2 minutes until golden brown. Remove from the oil, drain on absorbent paper, season with salt to serve.

Tip

Potatoes are a great thickening agent for soups. If you find your finished soup a bit on the thin side, add a very finely chopped raw potato to about 2 cups of soup and cook for 5 minutes until the potato is soft. Blend briefly in the processor using the double bladed knife then stir into the cooked soup.

PRALINE

Double bladed knife

Praline is made from caramelized sugar and almonds. It is delightful either in or on ice-cream, as a flavouring for cream for gateaux or as a sweet garnish. Place 175 g/6 oz granulated sugar and 175 g/6 oz almonds in a heavy saucepan and place over a gentle heat until the sugar melts, turning the nuts over in the mixture with a wooden spoon. Continue cooking in this manner until the mixture is a rich mid-brown. Transfer the mixture to a board covered with a piece of oiled foil; allow to cool. Break into pieces and add to the food processor and either chop or grind. Store in an airtight container until required. Makes about 225 g/8 oz.

PROCESS

This is the general term for running the food processor no what what blade, disc or attachment is fitted.

PULSE

Most food processors have a pulse features which allows the machine to run for just a second or two while your finger is depressing the switch. This is an invaluable feature as it allows you fine control over the machine and prevents food from becoming over-processed. Use whenever you are in doubt about how long a process takes or when the food is almost ready. It is particularly useful if the machine does not have variable speed control.

PUREE

This is the process of reducing food to a thick liquid. The most common purees are those of cooked vegetables which are then served as an accompaniment or used in recipes such as soups, sauces or pâtés, and fruit, either raw or cooked.

The process was traditionally done using a sieve and elbow grease but now the job is performed in a few seconds in the food processor fitted with the double bladed knife. Generally, remove the vegetables from the cooking liquid and process until smooth, then blend in cooking liquid to taste. Most fruits can be pureed raw and need no additional liquid.

See Fruit; individual Vegetable entries.

Q

QUICHES

Double bladed knife
Grating disc
Slicing disc

Cheese and Vegetable Quiche

Make 175 g/6 oz Shortcrust Pastry (see page 87) and use to line a 20 cm/8 in flan dish or flan tin with a removable base. Bake 'blind' in a preheated oven 200°C/400°F/gas 6 for 8–10 mintues, until firm; reduce the heat to 180°C/350°F/gas 4. Slightly beat an egg and brush the inside of the pastry with the egg, return to the oven for 3–4 minutes. This will seal the pastry and prevent it from becoming moist whilst cooking.

Prepare 450 g/1 lb vegetables, e.g. peppers, onions, celery, carrots, aubergines or leeks, using the slicing disc and cook as appropriate, either by frying gently in butter or margarine or by boiling. Cool the cooked vegetables and place in the pastry base. Grate 175 g/6 oz Gruyere, Cheddar or Caerphilly cheese (or combine different cheeses) using the grating disc and sprinkle over the vegetables. Break 2 eggs into the bowl fitted with the double bladed knife and add any egg left over from preparing the pastry base, then add 150 ml/¼ pint milk and 150 ml/¼ pint single cream, 1 × 5 ml spoon/ 1 tsp dried parsley and salt and pepper to taste. Process for 10 seconds then pour over the quiche. Arrange a few slices of tomato on the top if desired. Bake at 180°C/350°F/gas 4 for 35–40 minutes until set and golden.

Onion and Mushroom Quiche

Make the pastry and blind bake following the instructions above. Cut a medium onion in quarters, then process until very finely chopped using the double bladed knife. Heat 25 g/1 oz butter in a saucepan and add the onion, sweat over a very gentle heat for about 5 minutes. Meanwhile chop 225 g/8 oz flat mushrooms until very fine in the processor and then add to the onions with 1 × 15 ml spoon/1 tbsp white wine. Continue to cook over a very low heat, stirring frequently, for 20–30 minutes until all the liquid thrown off by the mushrooms has evaporated. Cool slightly and spoon into the pastry shell taking care to drain off any excess liquid that remains. While the mushroom mixture is cooking place the leftover egg from preparing the base, 1 more whole egg and 1 egg yolk into the bowl fitted with the double bladed knife. Add 300 ml/½ pint single cream, a generous pinch of nutmeg and salt and pepper to taste; process for 10 seconds to blend. Pour over the mushroom mixture and sprinkle over 1 × 15 ml spoon/ 1 tbsp Parmesan cheese. Bake for about 40 minutes until risen and slightly golden on the top.

R

RADISHES

Slicing disc

Slicing: Trim both ends of the radishes. Place the radishes in the feeder tube, stacking vertically if you desire evenly shaped slices. Process the slices using a firm pressure on the presser.

RASPBERRY

Double bladed knife

Puree: Raspberries are often pureed before using in souffles, mousses or sauces. For most purposes it is best to remove the seeds by passing the puree through a nylon sieve; do not use a metal sieve as they may flavour the raspberry mixture.

See Fruit.

Raspberry Sauce

This versatile sauce can be made savoury or sweet.

Puree 350 g/12 oz of raspberries in the food processor and pass through a nylon sieve. Place 100 g/4 oz red currant jelly in a small pan with 1 × 15 ml spoon/1 tbsp lemon juice. Heat gently until the jelly has melted. If serving the sauce hot add the raspberry puree to the pan and heat through. Taste and add pepper for a savoury sauce to serve with duck or pork, or a little icing sugar for a sweeter sauce to pour over poached pears or peaches. If serving cold, pour the melted jelly into the raspberry puree and sweeten to taste with icing sugar and leave to cool. Serve cold, not chilled, with ice cream or sorbet.

RATATOUILLE

Slicing disc
Double bladed knife

Slice 2 courgettes (see page 38) and 1 small aubergine (see page 17) cutting into pieces to fit the feeder tube. Sprinkle the vegetables with salt and leave for 30 minutes. Rinse in cold water to remove the salt and dry well with absorbent kitchen paper. Meanwhile, slice 2 medium onions, 2 small green peppers and 1 red pepper. Heat 4 × 15 ml spoons/4 tbsp olive oil in a large frying pan, add the onions and fry gently for 3–4 minutes to soften. Add 1 crushed clove of garlic and the sliced vegetables. Continue to cook turning the vegetables over in the oil occasionally, for about 10 minutes. Process 400 g/14 oz tinned tomatoes with the double bladed knife for 8–10 seconds until chopped, not pureed. Pour over the vegetables and add 2 × 15 ml spoons/2 tbsp white wine (optional), 1 × 5 ml spoon/1 tsp dried marjoram. Simmer for 20–30 minutes and serve hot, or cold as a salad.

RISSOLES

Double bladed knife

Roughly tear 4 slices of bread and place in the bowl fitted with the double bladed knife. Add 375 g/12 oz cooked meat cut into 2.5 cm/1 in cubes, 2 × 5 ml spoons/2 tsp marjoram, pinch of cayenne pepper and salt and pepper to taste. Process until crumbled. Lightly beat 1 egg with a fork and, with the motor running, pour half through the feeder tube and process for 2 seconds. Gradually add remaining egg, until the mixture binds together. Shape the mixture into small patties and lightly coat in flour. For a crisp coating, dip the floured patties in beaten egg and then in dry breadcrumbs. Shallow fry in 4–6 × 15 ml spoons/4–6 tbsp oil.

S

SALADS

Slicing disc
Grating disc
Double bladed knife

The food processor really comes into its own when preparing salads, whther for the family or for a crowd. The even slices enhance the appearance of the salad and the speed of processing cuts down the preparation time enormously. The majority of processors feed the sliced food directly into the bowl, but some have a funnel that directs the sliced ingredients into a bowl of your choice. If you make a lot of salads, or you make large quantities, this option is a boon.

Vegetable Pasta Salad

Cook 300 g/10 oz pasta shapes just tender, drain and rinse under cold water. Set aside. Fit the large grating or Julienne disc and process 1 large carrot and 2 sticks of celery. Fit the slicing disc and slice lengthways (see page 51) 100 g/4 oz French beans, 2 courgettes, ½ green and ½ red pepper and 3 spring onions. Place all the vegetables except the peppers and spring onions in boiling water and blanch for 3 minutes. Drain thoroughly, rinse under cold water and pat dry with absorbent paper. Toss together in a large bowl the pasta, cooked and raw vegetables. For the dressing, combine in the bowl fitted with the double bladed knife, 150 ml/¼ pint olive oil, 4 × 15 ml spoons/4 tbsp lemon juice, 1 × 5 ml spoon/1 tsp poppy seeds, few drops of Tabasco sauce, a pinch of sugar and salt and pepper to taste. Process for a few seconds then pour over the salad and toss. Leave for 1 hour in a cool place before serving.

Potato Salad

Cook 1 kg/2 lbs waxy potatoes until tender, drain and cool until warm. Meanwhile, with the double bladed knife, finely chop 1 bunch of chives, mint or parsley, add 150 ml/¼ pint mayonnaise, 4 × 15 ml spoons/4 tbsp plain yogurt, 1 × 15 ml spoon/1 tbsp Dijon mustard and salt and pepper to taste. Process for a few seconds to blend, remove the knife and insert the slicing disc. Slice the potatoes then slice 4 spring onions and 3 sticks of celery into the dressing. Place in a serving dish, turning the ingredients to ensure they are evenly covered in dressing. For a main course, slice Continental style sausages into the salad.

Grated Carrot Salad

With the double bladed knife fitted place 2 × 15 ml spoons each of sunflower oil, lemon juice, water and plain yogurt in the processor bowl and blend for a few seconds until amalgamated. Remove the double bladed knife and insert the grating disc. Grate 4 large carrots into the dressing. Using a spoon, stir 75 g/3 oz raisins, 100 g/4 oz peanuts and 2 × 15 ml spoons/2 tbsp sesame seeds. Turn into a serving bowl.

SALAD DRESSINGS

See Dressings; Mayonnaise.

SALMON

See Fish.

SANDWICH SPREADS

Slicing disc
Grating disc
Double bladed knife

Spring Onion and Red Pepper

Roughly chop 2 spring onions and ½ red pepper in the processor fitted with a double bladed knife. Add a 200 g/7 oz can drained tuna fish and 100 g/4 oz low fat soft cheese, pulse until combined.

Egg and Cheese

Cut 2 hard-boiled eggs into quarters, process until finely chopped. Add 4 gherkins or 1 dill pickle, ½ × 5 ml spoon/½ tsp paprika. Grate in 100 g/4 oz cheese and bind with 1 × 15 ml spoon/1 tbsp or more mayonnaise and/or yogurt.

SATAY SAUCE

Double bladed knife

The Indonesian dish satay, based on a spicy peanut sauce, has become very popular in recent years.

With the motor running and the double bladed knife fitted, drop a clove or garlic through the feeder tube. When chopped add a quartered onion and chop until fine. Add 4 × 15 ml spoons/4 tbsp each of peanut butter (see also page 81), ground nut or sunflower oil and soy sauce, 50 g/2 oz brown sugar, juice and rind of ½ lemon, 1 × 15 ml spoon/1 tbsp ground coriander, salt, pepper and cayenne pepper to taste. Pulse until well blended. Use as a Marinade for uncooked meat or poultry, then for basting while grilling or barbecuing the meat until tender. Sufficient for 750 g/1½ lbs meat or poultry.

SAUSAGES

Slicing disc

Slicing Ready-to-eat Sausages: Firm-textured salami-type sausages are most successful. The firmest sausages can be sliced at room temperature, but generally it is best to chill well first. Cut straight across into lengths to fit the feeder tube, place two or even three pieces in the tube at one time and process using a firm pressure on the pusher. Generally the medium or fine disc will be used but thicker slices may be good in stews or chunky salads.

Tip

A small amount of meat will inevitably stick to the slicing disc whilst in operation; however if a lot of meat is sticking and impeding the slicing operation it means that the sausage is not firm enough to process. In this case place in the freezer for a short time to chill further but do not allow to freeze solid.

SAUSAGE MEAT

Double bladed knife

Cut 225 g/8 oz belly pork and 225 g/8 oz lean pork into 2.5 cm/1 in pieces and place in the processor fitted with the double bladed knife. Add 1 × 5 ml spoon/1 tsp salt and ½ × 5 ml spoon/½ tsp each fresh parsley, sage and thyme. Process for about 15 seconds until the ingredients are very finely chopped.

SCONES

Double bladed knife

Place 225 g/8 oz self-raising flour ½ × 5 ml spoon/½ tsp salt and 25 g/1 oz caster sugar in the bowl and process for 3 seconds to sift. Add 50 g/2 oz diced cold butter and process for about 5 seconds until the mixture resembles fine breadcrumbs. With the motor running, pour in 150 ml/¼ pint milk or sufficient to form a soft dough. Turn the dough out onto a floured board and roll to a thickness of 1.5 cm/¾ in. Cut into 5 cm/2 in rounds, place on a greased baking sheet and brush the tops with a little milk. Cook at 220°C/425°F/gas 7 for 10–12 minutes until risen and golden.

Cheese Scones

Add a generous pinch of cayenne pepper and dry mustard and some freshly ground black pepper to the flour. Then mix 40 g/1½ oz mature Cheddar cheese before adding the milk.

Fruit Scones

Add a pinch of mixed spice or grated nutmeg with the flour, then 50 g/2 oz sultanas and 15 g/½ oz mixed peel as the dough begins to form.

SHORTBREAD

Double bladed knife

Process together 100 g/4 oz soft butter and 50 g/2 oz caster sugar until light and fluffy – about 20 seconds depending on the softness of the butter. Add 150 g/5 oz plain flour and 50 g/2 oz rice flour and pulse until mixed together to form a dough. Press into a greased and lined 18 cm/7 in round tin and prick the surface all over. Flute the edges with the fingers and mark into 8 wedges. Bake at 160°C/325°F/gas 3 for about 40 minutes until firm and a pale straw colour. Leave for 5 minutes, cut into the triangles and cool on a wire rack.

Strawberry Shortbread

Make 1 quantity of shortbread but do not cut throughthe cooked shortbread. Wipe and hull 225 g/8 oz strawberries, slice in half (see page 112), stir into 150 ml/ ¼ pint whipped cream (sweetened if desired with icing sugar). Pile on top of the cold shortbread. Decorate with the remaining whole strawberries and fresh mint leaves.

SLICE

One of the basic functions of the food processor. Many machines come with a selection of slicing discs as standard, others have a variable blade which enables you to alter the thickness of a single slicing disc. The discs are fitted on a central pole which spins when the machine is turned on. The speed and sharpness of the blades enable fast and even slicing. For machines with variable speeds, slice hard foods such as carrots, potatoes and cheese at a fast speed and slow speeds for soft fruits such as strawberries and kiwi.

General guidelines for slicing:

☆ Pack the food evenly in the feeder tube.
☆ Apply an even pressure on the pusher.
☆ Select ripe, but firm fruit.
☆ Chill cheese and meats before slicing.
☆ Cut a slice from the food to produce a flat edge upon which to begin slicing.
☆ Empty the bowl when nearly full. Many machines have a line marked on the machine to indicate that it is full, but as a general guide, empty before the food in the bowl reaches within 1 cm/½ in of the slicing disc.

SOUFFLE

See Eggs.

SORBET

Double bladed knife
Whisk attachment

This recipe is a guide; substitute fruits of your choice.

Mango Sorbet

Place the flesh from 2 mangos (approximately 450 g/ 1 lb) in the bowl and process until very smooth. Add the grated rind and juice of 1 lemon and icing sugar to taste. Process until blended. Transfer to a shallow container and allow to freeze – about 4 hours. Whisk 1 egg white until stiff and set aside (optional). Return the double bladed knife to the bowl (without washing), break the sorbet into chunks and place in the bowl. Process until smooth but do not allow to thaw completely. If adding egg whites, place in the bowl with the sorbet and pulse until the mixture is just blended. Place in a covered container and freeze for about 6 hours before serving.

SOUPS

Double bladed knife

A food processor is a must for anyone who frequently makes soups. It can chop, slice or even grate all the vegetables before they are added to the pan for cooking and then puree the resulting soup in next to no time. Cook the soup ingredients together as usual then, once the soup is cooked, transfer the vegetable pieces from the pan to the work bowl using a slotted spoon, so the double bladed knife will have something solid to cut into. Puree the soup and return to the liquid in the pan; stir well to mix and reheat.

Italian Brown Bean Soup

Slice a medium onion, then fry gently in 3 × 15 ml spoons/3 tbsp oil until soft. Meanwhile, slice 225 g/8 oz potatoes, add to the pan with 1 litre/2 pints beef stock and simmer for 15–20 minutes until the potato is soft. Transfer the vegtables to the processor bowl using a slotted spoon and leaving most of the liquid behind. Process for 15–20 seconds until the potato and onion are pureed. Return to the saucepan with 225 g/8 oz diced potato, 1 400 g/14 oz drained can brown beans, 1 × 15 ml spoons/1 tbsp tomato puree and 2 × 15 ml spoons/2 tbsp freshly chopped parsley. Season with salt and pepper to taste and simmer for about 15 minutes until the potatoes are tender, stirring occasionally to prevent the soup from burning on the base of the pan.

Creamy Tomato Soup

Finely chop a handful of fresh basil or chives using the double bladed knife, then, without removing the herbs finely chop a medium-sized onion; place in a saucepan. Skin 1.2 kg/2½ lbs ripe tomatoes and remove the seeds (do this holding the tomatoes over a sieve so that the juices are caught in the pan). Add to the saucepan the tomato flesh, 1 litre/2/pints vegetable stock, 1 × 5 ml spoon/1 tsp sugar and salt and pepper to taste. Bring to the boil and simmer for 15–20 minutes until the onion and tomato are soft. Place in the processor bowl (in 2 batches if necessary) and process until very smooth. Add 150 ml/¼ pint single cream and process until well blended. Return to a clean pan to heat through but do not boil.

SPEED CONTROL

Some processors have a variable speed control which allows you more control over the speed at which food is processed and allows the motor to draw on more power for heavy tasks such as bread making than for slicing tomatoes. The manufacturer's handbook will provide details on which speeds to use for which processes; the instructions in this book have been written assuming that this feature is not available.

SPICES

Do not attempt to grind spices in the food processor as the quantities are too small and the seeds themselves are usually too hard.

SPINACH PUREE

Double bladed knife

Wash the spinach well, discard the stalks, and large ribs, if necessary, and tear into large pieces. Place in a saucepan, cover and cook with no additional water. Lift the lid and stir frequently. Once the spinach has completely wilted it will be cooked in about 2 minutes. Drain well and cool slightly. Place in the bowl fitted with the double bladed knife and process until smooth, about 10 seconds, scraping down the sides of the bowl once. Return to the pan and cook, uncovered until all the liquid has boiled off. Stir in a knob of butter, a sprinkling of grated nutmeg and salt and pepper to taste. For a creamy spinach puree, add about 90 ml/3 fl oz single cream with nutmeg, salt and pepper to taste.

Pureed spinach can also be used in souffles, roulades, as a filling for pancakes, or as a basis for soup, simply add milk and stock to the puree.

SPONGE CAKES

See Cakes.

SPONGE PUDDING

Double bladed knife

Make your favourite sponge pudding recipe in the food processor using either the creaming method or the all-in-one method (see Cakes).

Tip
If making all-in-one cake-type recipes, use soft rather than hard margarine as it blends quicker.

Orange Sponge Pudding

Place in the processor bowl 100 g/4 oz each of caster sugar and soft margarine, 150 g/6 oz self-raising flour, 1 × 5 ml spoon/1 tsp each of grated orange rind and cinnamon, 2 eggs and 2 × 15 ml spoons/2 tbsp orange juice. Process for 10 seconds, scrape down the sides of the bowl and process for a further 10 seconds, until smooth. Place 4 × 15 ml spoons/4 tbsp marmalade in the bottom of a greased 1.5 litre/2½ pint basin and top with the sponge mixture. Cover with greaseproof paper and a pudding cloth and steam over gently boiling water for 2 hours. Top up the water level occasionally. Alternatively, omit pudding cloth and cook in the microwave on HIGH for 5–8 minutes until the top is just set. Leave to stand for 5 minutes.

SPRING ONIONS

Slicing disc
Double bladed knife

Slicing: Trim the onions into lengths to fit the feeder tube and insert vertically, packing them in tightly. Place the pusher in position and slice, using a moderate pressure on the pusher. For long lengthwise slices, cut into lengths to fit the length of the feeder tube and insert horizontally. Slice using a gentle pressure on the pusher. For both types of slices the medium slicing disc is usually adequate although the thin disc may be used.

Chopping: Use the bowl fitted with the double bladed knife. Cut into 2.5 cm/1 in pieces and process using the pulse method until the desired texture is achieved. Use in salads, sandwich fillings, omlettes, souffles and casseroles.

STIR FRY

Double bladed knife

The processor is a Godsend if you like stir-fry dishes which require vegetables and meat to be finely sliced so that they will cook quickly in hot oil. The medium slicing disc is usually satisfactory for all the vegetables; slice them in groups of the same density, then empty the bowl before starting on the next group.

Meat and poultry can be sliced in a semi-frozen state into thin slices but do not attempt to slice unfrozen meat – cut with a sharp knife across the grain if you have not time to part-freeze (see Meat for more details).

Stir-fried Chicken and Onions

Semi-freeze 3 chicken breasts then slice (see page 34). Place in a bowl. Combine 3 × 15 ml spoons/3 tbsp each of soy sauce and Worcestershire sauce, 4 slices of root ginger and 1 clover of garlic. Pour over the chicken, stir to coat then leave until completely thawed, turning the chicken from time to time.

Slice 8 spring onions and half a red pepper lengthwise (see pages 111 and 91). Heat the 2 × 15 ml spoons/2 tbsp oil in a wok or large heavy frying pan and add the spring onions and pepper, stir-fry for 1–2 minutes until tender but still firm. Remove from the pan and keep warm. Add the drained chicken to the wok and stir-fry for 2–3 minutes until the chicken slices are cooked through. Add 3 × 15 ml spoons/3 tbsp water to the remaining marinade and mix with 1 × 5 ml spoon/ 1 tsp cornflour which has been mixed to a paste with a little water. Return the spring onions and peppers to the pan. Pour over the marinade mixture and cook, stirring, until the sauce thickens slightly; add more soy sauce, salt and pepper to taste.

STRAWBERRIES

Double bladed knife
Slicing disc

To slice strawberries, select fruit that is ripe but firm, place in the feeder tube, positioning horizontally, if uniform slices are required, and process with a very light pressure on the pusher.

Strawberries, like other soft fruits, can be pureed without adding extra liquid because of their high water content. Process 375–450 g/¾–1 lb at a time, depending on the capacity of your machine and sweeten to taste with a little sifted icing sugar if desired. Use as a sauce with poached fruit, ice-cream or as the basis for drinks such as strawberry milkshake (see Milkshakes) or Strawberry Juice.

Strawberry Juice Drink
Puree 450 g/1 lb strawberries, add juice of 1 lemon, 450 ml/¾ pint boiling water and 150 ml/¼ pint orange juice and leave to cool. Chill before serving.

Strawberry Daiquiri
Place in the processor fitted with a double bladed knife, 100 g/4 oz strawberries, 75 ml/2½ fl oz white rum,

1 × 15 ml spoon/1 tbsp lemon juice, 1 × 15 ml spoon strawberry milkshake syrup or grenadine. Process until smooth, then pour over crushed ice.

See also Strawberry Souffle page 47.

STUFFING

Double bladed knife

For a basic stuffing, place a small bunch of parsley and sage (if available) in the bowl and process until finely chopped with the double bladed knife. Cut a small onion into quarters and a stick of celery (with leaves) into 2.5 cm/1 in pieces and add to bowl with ½ × 5 ml spoon/½ tsp salt, (1–2 × 5 ml spoon/1–2 tsp each of dried parsley and sage if fresh unavailable), freshly ground black pepper and 225 g/8 oz (about 8 slices) of bread torn into pieces. Process until the bread is crumbled, add a little boiling water or beaten egg down the feed tube to hold the stuffing together if required.

Mushroom Stuffing
Chop 75 g/3 oz mushrooms with the onion.

Nut Stuffing
Add 75 g/3 oz chopped nuts to the finished stuffing.

SUGAR

Double bladed knife

Make caster sugar from granulated sugar by placing the required amount of the latter in the bowl and process until the required texture is achieved. This is slightly more powdery than purchased caster sugar but is a more than adequate substitute.

SWEDES

Slicing disc

Cut about 450 g/1 lb peeled swede into pieces to fit the feeder tube and slice using a firm pressure on the pusher. Cook in slightly salted boiling water for about 15 minutes, until tender. Drain well. If serving sliced, toss in melted butter seasoned with nutmeg and black pepper. To puree, allow the swede to cool slightly, then place in the processor fitted with the double bladed knife with 40 g/1½ oz butter, pinch of nutmeg and salt and black pepper to taste, and process until smooth. For a puree with more colour, add a cooked carrot.

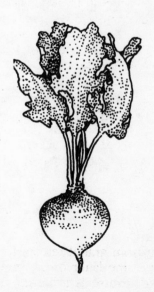

T

TARAMASALATA

Double bladed knife

Place 100 g/4 oz skinned cod's roe in the bowl fitted with the double bladed knife and process 10–15 seconds until smooth. Add 2 medium-sized cooked potatoes and blend again until smooth. With the motor running, add 120 ml/4 fl oz olive oil down the feed tube. Stop the machine and add the juice of 1 lemon, 1 × 15 ml spoon/1 tbsp white wine vinegar and about 2 × 15 ml spoon/2 tbsp water. Pulse to mix, then taste and add a little more lemon juice and/or vinegar to taste depending on the strength of the cod's roe. If the taramasalata is too thick add a little more water.

TOMATO

Slicing disc
Double bladed knife

To slice tomatoes, select firm tomatoes, cut in half lengthwise to fit the feeder tube and make a straight cut to form a flat cutting surface. Insert either through the top or base of the feeder whichever is easiest. Process using a gentle pressure on the pusher.

To chop tomatoes, skin and remove the seeds if desired then cut in quarters, or for large tomatoes in wedges and process using the double bladed knife until of the desired texture. Process about 4 medium tomatoes at one time, or 1 very large beefsteak tomato.

Tomato and Mozzarella Salad

Chop the leaves from 2–3 sprigs of basil using the double bladed knife, remove the knife and fit the slicing disc. Slice 2 medium beefsteak tomatoes and arrange on

4 individual serving plates. Sprinkle with the basil. Rinse the bowl and blade, then slice 2 chilled Mozzarella cheeses (see page 32). Interleave with the tomatoes. Drizzle over olive oil mixed with a little white wine vinegar and season with salt and black pepper.

Tomato Sauce

This is a good basic sauce that can be used as an accompaniment or as the basis of a pasta sauce. Canned tomatoes may be used in place of the fresh, especially when the flavour of fresh tomatoes is not so strong.

With the motor running and the double bladed knife fitted, drop a clove of garlic through the feed tube and process until chopped. Add a small, quartered onion and finely chop. Heat 2 × 15 ml spoons/2 tbsp olive oil in a pan and add the onion and garlic and cook over a gentle heat until soft. Meanwhile, skin 450 g/1 lb tomatoes and remove the seeds, if desired. Cut the tomatoes into quarters then process until chopped; or use a 400 g/14 oz can of tomatoes, drained. Add to the pan with the onions. Add 60 ml/2 fl oz red wine, 1 × 5 ml spoon/1 tsp chopped dried basil or parsley, 1 bay leaf, a large pinch of sugar and salt and pepper to taste. Simmer the sauce for about 15 minutes until thickened. For a smooth sauce, do not peel and deseed tomatoes but pass the finished sauce through a sieve.

Tomato Relish

With the motor running and the double bladed knife fitted, drop 2 cloves of garlic through the feed tube and process until chopped. Add a Spanish onion, cut into chunks, 1 large peeled and cored cooking apple and process until finely chopped; transfer to a large saucepan. Peel and deseed 1 kg/2 lb tomatoes, add to the processor bowl and chop finely; add to the saucepan with 225 g/8 oz brown sugar, 1 × 5 ml spoon/1 tsp each of salt and paprika pepper, a pinch of cayenne pepper and 450 ml/¾ pint white vinegar. Bring to the boil and cook for about 20 minutes until all the ingredients are reduced to a pulpy texture. Place in warmed clean jars and seal.

TUNA FISH

See Fish for general treatment.

Pollo Tonnato

This is a classic Italian dish in which tuna mayonnaise is used to coat poached chicken.

Poach 4 boned and skinned chicken breasts in 150 ml/¼ pint each water and white wine, a bay leaf and a few peppercorns for about 20 minutes.

Meanwhile, place 2 egg yolks and the juice of ½ lemon in the bowl fitted with the double bladed knife and process for about 10 seconds, until well blended. With the motor running slowly pour through the feed tube 300 ml/½ pint olive oil. Once thickened add 200 g/7 oz well-drained can tuna fish, a little freshly ground black pepper, 4 anchovy fillets and a few capers. Process until smooth, then add a little of the poaching liquid to thin the sauce to a spreading consistency. Place the drained chicken breasts on a serving plate and while still warm pour over the sauce, coating each piece of chicken thoroughly. Allow to cool then cover and place in the refrigerator for a couple of hours before serving.

TURKEY

See Chicken.

TURNIP

Treat as for Swedes.

V

VEGETABLES

Slicing disc
Double bladed knife

See individual entries.

Italian Vegetables

An unusual way to prepare vegetables, they are sliced and baked in a hot oven in plenty of rich olive oil. Each retains its own individual flavour while taking on a hint of its neighbour's.

Fit the slicing disc and slice 2 courgttes and half an aubergine, sprinkle with salt and leave for 30 minutes, rinse in cold water and pat dry with absorbent paper. Slice 3–4 medium potatoes. Place in slightly salted, cold water and bring to the boil, simmer for a few minutes, then drain and set aside. Slice 1 small red and 1 small green pepper and 2 tomatoes. Lay the vegetables in strips in a roasting tin and sprinkle over a little salt and freshly ground black pepper. Pour 4 × 15 ml spoons/ 4 tbsp olive oil over the vegetables. Place in a pre-heated oven 200°C/400°F/gas 6 for 30 minutes until all the vegetables are tender, basting twice. Serve with roast meats or as a dish for vegetarians.

Vegetable Curry

With the motor running and the double bladed knife fitted, drop a clove of garlic down the feed tube and process until chopped. Cut a medium onion in quarters and add to the bowl and chop. Heat 50 g/2 oz ghee or butter in a large pan and add the onion and 1 × 5 ml spoon/1 tsp cumin seeds, saute gently until soft. Meanwhile, slice 4 small potatoes, 1 small aubergine, 1 green pepper and 2 carrots. Stir into the onion mixture, 1 × 5 ml spoon/1 tsp each of salt, turmeric, ground coriander and chilli and fry for 1 minute. Add the sliced vegetables and turn in the flavoured fat. Roughly chop 4 large tomatoes or 1 400 g/14 oz can using the double bladed knife and pour over the vegetables with 90 ml/3 fl oz water. Bring to the boil, cover and simmer for 20–30 minutes until all the vegetables are tender adding a handful of frozen peas 5 minutes before the vegetables are cooked. Serve garnished with chopped fresh coriander leaves.

VICTORIA SPONGE CAKE

See Cakes.

W

WALNUTS

Double bladed knife

For general treatment see Nuts, bearing in mind that walnuts are a particularly oily nut.

Walnut Pasta Sauce

Roughly chop 75 g/3 oz walnuts using the double bladed knife. Heat 150 ml/¼ pint single cream in a saucepan and add 175 g/6 oz crumbled Gorgonzola cheese. When melted, add the walnuts and season to taste with salt and black pepper. Serve over 350 g/12 oz cooked noodles. Sprinkle with grated Parmesan cheese (see page 32).

WATERCRESS

Double bladed knife

Chopping: Discard the thick stalks and chop the leaves using the double bladed knife. Chopped watercress can be used to flavour mayonnaise for serving with fish, mixed with cheese for a delicious souffle, and is good in quiches and omelettes.

WELSH RAREBIT

Double bladed knife

Chop 100 g/4 oz cheese into 2.5 cm/1 in cubes and process using the double bladed knife until crumbled. Add 4 × 15 ml spoons/4 tbsp each of beer and single cream or milk, ½ × 5 ml spoon/½ tsp dry mustard, 15 g/½ oz butter, a generous pinch of cayenne pepper and salt to taste. Process for a few seconds, scrape down the sides of the bowl and process until mixed. Toast 4 slices of thickly cut bread on one side. Spread the cheese mixture on the untoasted side and return to the grill until the cheese mixture is bubbling and golden brown.

WHIP

This is one of the processes the early food processors did not perform, and even today the whisk attachment is often an optional accessory that is purchased separately. Plastic and double bladed knives can add sufficient air to half whip cream, but they will not whisk egg whites for meringues or souffles. If you require cream to fill a gateau or to top a trifle, then the plastic or double bladed knife will do the job adequately, but you will not be able to pipe the cream as it will not hold its shape well. The pusher should not be in the feeder tube when whipping.

WHISK ATTACHMENT

This attachment is sometimes a paddle-like attachment or flat disc that fits in position like the basic knife, or it is a traditional whisk which is suspended from the lid of the processor. As the basic food processor is incapable of whisking eggs, egg whites or cream until very thick, this attachment is very useful. Do not have the pusher in the feeder tube when whisking.

WHITE SAUCE

See Bechamel Sauce.

Y

YAM

Double bladed knife
Slicing disc

Yams can be treated in almost the same way as ordinary potatoes, although their taste is quite different.
Slicing: Cut into wedges to fit the feed tube, then process using a moderate pressure on the pusher.

Baked Candied Yams

Parboil unpeeled yams for 10 minutes, cool slightly and peel. Slice the yams as directed above and place in a buttered ovenproof dish. In a small saucepan place 25 g/1 oz butter, the grated rind and 3 × 15 ml spoons/ 3 tbsp orange juice, 2 × 15 ml spoons/2 tbsp soft brown sugar and ½ × 5 ml spoon/½ tsp ground ginger. Heat gently until the butter has melted and the sugar dissolved, bring to the boil and pour over the yams. Bake in an oven preheated to 180°C/350°F/gas 4 for about 30 minutes until the yams are tender, basting occasionally with the orange syrup. This dish is good with plain cooked fish or meat kebabs.

YEAST DOUGHS

Double bladed knife
Plastic knife
Dough hook

Kneading by hand usually takes about 10 minutes of quite hard work, which puts many people off. Kneading in the food processor takes just a few seconds and the resulting bread has an excellent even texture (see page 63).

> ### Tip
> If making yeast mixtures with added dried fruit, use the dough hook or plastic blade to prevent it from being chopped as the sharp double bladed knife will cut the fruit into tiny pieces. If you have to use the sharp knife, then add the fruit after the dough has been kneaded and pulse until just mixed.

Read the manufacturer's handbook before beginning a recipe as it is important not to exceed the capacity of your machine or the motor may be damaged. As the process is so quick, it is easy to divide the mixture into two batches and process them separately then knead them together by hand.

Hot Cross Buns

With the plastic knife fitted, add to the bowl 1 × 15 ml spoon/1 tbsp dried yeast, 1 × 5 ml spoon/1 tsp sugar, 150 ml/¼ pint warm milk, 120 ml/4 fl oz warm water and 100 g/4 oz plain flour. Process for 5 seconds, scrape down the sides of the bowl and process for another 5 seconds, set aside to rise in a warm place for about 30 minutes, until doubled in bulk.

Place 350 g/12 oz plain flour, 1 × 5 ml spoon/1 tsp salt, ½ × 5 ml spoon each of mixed spice, cinnamon and nutmeg and 50 g/2 oz caster sugar. Process for 5 seconds to sift. Into the yeast mixture stir in 1 beaten egg and 50 g/2 oz melted butter, then pour into the flour mixture. Knead in the processor until the mixture forms a ball – about 45 seconds.

Add 100 g/4 oz currants and 25 g/1 oz mixed peel and pulse to blend. Divide the dough into 12–16 buns, then place well spaced out on a floured baking sheet. Cover with oiled plastic food wrap and leave to rise in a warm place for 45 minutes or until doubled in size. Cut a cross on each bun using a sharp knife and bake at 200°C/400°F/gas 6 for 15–20 minutes until golden brown. Cool on a wire rack. To glaze the buns, combine 2 × 15 ml spoons/2 tbsp milk with 3½ × 15 ml spoons/3½ tbsp sugar and heat until the sugar is dissolved, bring to the boil and boil for 2 minutes. Brush the hot buns twice with the glaze.

See Bread; Knead.

INDEX OF RECIPES

Apple Sauce, 16
Apple Scones, 17
Apricot and Brazil Nut Cake, 80
Aubergines Parmigiana, 17

Baked Candied Yams, 123
Banana Milk Shake, 74
Blue Cheese Dressing, 44
Buttercream, 60

Caramelized Oranges, 85
Cheat's Pâté, 89
Cheese and Vegetable Quiche, 98
Cheese Scones, 106
Cheesy Supper Bake, 33
Chicken Liver Pâté, 89
Chocolate Milk Shake, 74
Choux Pastry, 88
Coleslaw, 27
Courgette Pancakes, 39
Cream Cheese Frosting, 60
Creamy Cashew Dip, 43
Creamy Tomato Soup, 109
Crisps, 95
Crunchy Oat Biscuits, 23
Cucumber Dip, 41

Dhal, 67
Dundee Marmalade, 69

Egg and Cheese Spread, 104
Egg Salad, 47

French Onion Soup, 83
Fruit Puree, 51
Fruit Scones, 106
Fudge Icing, 60

Garlic Bread, 53
Ginger Marinade, 54
Grated Carrot Salad, 103
Guacamole, 18

Ham Sandwich Filler, 73
Hamburgers, 72
Herby Yogurt Dressing, 44
Horseradish Sauce, 58
Hot Cross Buns, 124
Humus, 35

Italian Vegetables, 119
Italian Brown Bean Soup, 109

Lemon Sauce Pudding, 67
Light Fruit Cake, 29

Mango Sorbet, 108
Manhattan Cheesecake, 33
Mint Sauce, 75
Mushroom Flan, 78
Mushroom and Spring Onion Omelette, 82

Normandy Tart, 16
Nut Rissoles, 80

Onion and Mushroom Quiche, 99
Orange Sponge Pudding, 111

Orange and Lemon Mousse, 76
Orange and Olive Salad, 84
Orange Protein Cup, 85

Pâté Sucree
  see Rich Sweet Pastry
Peach Melba, 90
Pease Pudding, 90
Pollo Tonnato, 118
Potato Salad, 103
Potatoes Dauphinois, 94

Quick Peach Ice-cream, 59

Raspberry Sauce, 100
Rich Vanilla Ice-cream, 59
Rich Sweet Pastry, 88
Rissoles, 101

Sauce Maltaise, 57
Sausage Meat, 105
Shortcrust Pastry, 87
Shortbread, 106
Sour Cream and Honey
  Dressing, 44
Spiced Apple Cake, 16
Spicy Peach and Plum Jam, 61

Spring Onion and Red
  Pepper Spread, 104
Stir-fried Chicken and
  Onions, 113
Strawberry Shortcake, 107
Strawberry Daiquiri, 112
Strawberry Juice Drink, 112
Strawberry Souffle, 47
Suet Pastry, 88
Sweet Souffle Omelette, 82
Swiss Rosti, 95
Swiss Roll, 28

Three Pepper Stew, 92
Tomato Relish, 117
Tomato and Mozzarella
  Salad, 116
Tomato Sauce, 117
Tuna Dip, 43
Two Salmon Mousse, 49

Vegetable Curry, 120
Vegetable Pasta Salad, 102
Victoria Sponge Cake, 28

Walnut Pasta Sauce, 121
Welsh Rarebit, 121
Wholemeal Pastry, 87

The Family Matters series:

A-Z of Childhood Illnesses 0 7063 6969 6
Anniversary Celebrations 0 7063 6636 0
Aromatherapy 0 7063 6959 9
Baby's First Year 0 7063 6778 2
Baby's Names 0 7063 6542 9
Baby's Names and Star Signs 0 7063 6801 0
Barbecue Tips 0 7063 6893 2
Card & Conjuring Tricks 0 7063 6811 8
Card Games 0 7063 6635 2
Card Games for One 0 7063 6747 2
Card Games for Two 0 7063 6907 6
Catering for a Wedding 0 7063 6953 X
Charades and Party Games 0 7063 6637 9
Children's Party Games 0 7063 6611 5
Christmas Planner 0 7063 6949 1
Common Ailments Cured Naturally 0 7063 6895 9
Does it Freeze? 0 7063 6960 2
Dreams and Their Meanings 0 7063 6802 9
Early Learning Games 0 7063 6771 5
First Time Father 0 7063 6952 1
Handwriting Secrets Revealed 0 7063 6841 X
How to be a Bridesmaid 0 7063 7003 1
How to be the Best Man 0 7063 6748 0
Microwave Tips & Timings 0 7063 6812 6
Modern Etiquette 0 7063 6641 7
Naming Baby 0 7063 5854 6
Palmistry 0 7063 6894 0
Preparing for Baby 0 7063 6883 5
Pressure Cooker Tips & Timings 0 7063 6908 4
Successful Children's Parties 0 7063 6843 6
Tracing Your Family Tree 0 7063 6947 5
Travel Games 0 7063 6643 3
Vegetarian Cooking Made Easy 0 7063 6941 6
Wedding Etiquette 0 7063 6868 1
Wedding Planner, The 0 7063 6867 3
Wedding Speeches and Toasts 0 7063 6642 5